# Raising Godly Tomatoes

by L. Elizabeth Krueger
a mother of ten (so far)

Raising Godly Tomatoes, Third Edition
Published by Krueger Publishing, Detroit, MI
Printed by Malloy Incorporated, Ann Arbor, MI
ISBN 978-0-9834842-0-2
Library of Congress Control Number: 2009278575
www.RaisingGodlyTomatoes.com



This book can also be found under the following ISBN numbers:
Previous editions: 978-1-60530-330-7
Hardcover edition: 978-0-9834842-1-9

# Dedication

*This book is dedicated to our ten beloved children, in whom we delight, in the hope that it will help them to raise "godly tomatoes" of their own. I would also like to thank Dr. James Juroe for his invaluable help in the editing of this manuscript.*

# CONTENTS

# WHY DO YOU HAVE SO MANY CHILDREN?

My husband and I have ten children. Ten so far, anyway. Large families being so rare today, I'm often asked, "Why would you want so many?" My answer is not typical of the other common "large family" rationales I've heard. You see, we didn't always want a lot of children. Neither were we compelled early on, by the conviction that in order to be obedient to God, we *must* have a large family. Rather, our desires and convictions evolved over time, through study, reflection, experience, and the godly advice of others.

Before marriage, I never bothered much with babies or children. I seldom played with dolls, rarely babysat, and was generally uncomfortable around children. Ignorant of how to handle them, I simply avoided them. I had, however, enjoyed my relationship with my own five siblings, and that experience perhaps conditioned me to the notion that the normative or "ideal" family was large.

Although from a smaller family, my husband's experiences and perceptions were not materially different from my own. So when we married, we decided on a nice neat two children, to be followed, perhaps, by a second pair after the first were both in school. After all, four at home simultaneously seemed to promise hopeless chaos and mental distress. Certainly more than I felt I could ever handle comfortably.

Then our first-born arrived, initiating new and wonderful ideas about love and family. Here was God's masterpiece—perfection in miniature! The creative genius was soon displayed again, this time in a girl displaying all the perfections of her older brother. Already, I envisioned her bedecked in smocked dresses, her little fingers playing the violin.

Slowly, but inexorably, our plan to wait until our first two were in school before having more began to change. Overwhelmed by the wonder, richness, and beauty that children had brought us, we abandoned the two now, two later plan. In short order we were soon welcoming our third and contemplating a fourth!

All was not bliss however. Parenting preschoolers proved difficult and frustrating. Despite the advice of numerous books and classes, I was confused, discouraged, and sometimes driven to the brink of despair by the myriad of annoyances and challenges presented each new day. What was acceptable behavior in a toddler and what should I be correcting? How was I to know where to draw lines and set the boundaries? What should I discipline them for and by what methods should I discipline? Clearly, I was struggling. I wanted to preserve the loving bond I had had with my babies, yet I didn't want to end up with spoiled, self-centered children that neither I nor anyone else could stand.

Then, as they grew a bit, I started worrying about their salvation. With so little control over their behavior, how could I hope to influence their hearts? I couldn't endure the thought that even one of my children might not become a believer. Given the risk of disbelief and rebellion, should we just continue along the same path as everyone else? Was it really enough to simply say we were "doing our best and trusting God with the rest" (the lame disclaimer of too many Christians whose rebellious children have been snared by the evil one)? Should we even have any more children, thereby tempting fate further than we already had?

Eventually the anxious fears and anxieties of these early years began to find resolution with three major life discoveries—a way to avoid wrong influences upon our children, a real life example to follow and ask counsel from, and a door to the Scriptures themselves revealing the great wealth of parenting advice they contain.

The first of these three discoveries was homeschooling. This afforded us the consoling hope that at age five, our children would not be thrust into the embraces and tutelage of a secular world whose end leads to destruction. Here was the perfect mechanism by which the pressures and negative influences of the world could be forestalled, allowing us to retain the loyalty and devotion of our children during their formative years. Homeschooling offered the bright hope that by keeping them close to us a while longer, we could knit their hearts to ours and also nurture them in the love of our omnipotent Creator.

Secondly, we started fellowshipping with a couple whose family impressed us as being what we wanted for our own family. Their children had grown from infancy to maturity with none of the behavioral tempests nowadays taken for granted and even expected. There were no temper tantrums, terrible twos, teenaged rebellion, raging hormones, drug usage, or promiscuity. Even the oldest children in this family maintained a close and loving relationship with their parents and the entire family loved and served God.

As we began to solicit this couple's parenting advice (much of which appears in this book), we saw that we really could raise obedient, godly children who would not go astray. There is great, liberating peace in realizing that God gives us a comprehensive plan. We don't have to just roll the dice. With this, we began, for the first time, to trust in God's words found in *Proverbs 22:6*, that if we *"train up a child in the way he should go, even when he is old he will not depart from it."*

The third major discovery was the enormous wealth of counsel and instruction the Bible contains about childrearing. The entire Bible is about children and families! The Bible is addressed to His children, *"the sheep of his pasture."* His promises and wisdom are directed to His children. He valued His children enough to die for them. Here in Scripture was the shaping vision that opened our eyes and stimulated us to the desire for more children. The Biblical model for discipline, training, and nurturing children enabled us to see that children are indeed the most precious gift the Lord bestows. We can now testify joyfully to the promise of the Psalmist that they are blessed whose *"quiver is full of them."*

And who wouldn't fervently desire more of such blessings? *"Behold, children are a gift of the LORD; the fruit of the womb is a reward." - Psalms 127:3*

*"Women should not have children after 35.*
*Thirty-five children are enough." - anonymous*

# Part I

# Underlying Principles

*My husband always had a handle on parenting and often tried to give me insight and help, but I just didn't get it. The first day I implemented your simple techniques, my husband came home from work – we were eating dinner – and he said, "Who are you people? Am I in the right house?" The change was that dramatic. Again, thank you.*

**Suzanne**

# one

# PREREQUISITES

*Blessed is the man whom You chasten, O LORD,*
*And whom You teach out of Your law.*
*- Psalms 94:12*

## Four Trouble Spots

I know your urge is to skip right to the "how to" section of this book, but please pause here for a few minutes first—I'll try to keep it short—and take time to ponder a few of the problems I run into over and over again as I speak to parents about their families. Failures in parenting today can frequently be traced to the following four underlying areas: (1) what your priorities are, (2) what your beliefs are regarding authority, (3) how willing you are to separate your children from the world, and (4) your willingness to reject worldly parenting theories and adopt biblical principles and godly standards instead.

*Children, be obedient to your parents in all things, for this is well-pleasing to the Lord.*
*- Colossians 3:20*

## Your Priorities As a Parent

I recently read about a woman who, after trying unsuccessfully to conceive for some years, adopted several small children. She had longed for children and dreamed of being a wonderful mother and enjoying parenthood. With these adoptions, she entered with excited anticipation down this bright path. Years later, after her children were grown, she confessed to an acquaintance that she had not enjoyed her journey at all. In fact, she had come to hate motherhood and was relieved when it was finally over. How sad. I really wonder what this poor lady's imaginary picture of motherhood had been when she first brought these children home. In all likelihood, she pictured in her mind's eye all the fun things that little girls imagine when they are playing with their dolls and more: cooing infants who love to be rocked to sleep, cute toddlers who enjoy playing peacefully for hours with blocks and toy trains, grade school children who are always eager to learn and never bicker, helpful teens who look forward to sharing confidences with Mom and Dad, and finally young adults who are mature and trustworthy and prepared to start families of their own.

Now I personally don't believe this picture is completely unrealistic. I have experienced all these things with my own children. However, it is only a partial picture. If you think that life will be like this all day every day with minimal effort on your part, think again. It won't be. This fantasy can become reality over time, but only with consistent, diligent effort on your part. You cannot enjoy the pleasures of a close, loving relationship with godly, well-behaved children if you are not willing to make parenting them your top priority. You must view it as your FULL TIME JOB, all day, every day. If you make it so, you will experience these rewards far sooner and in greater quantity that you could have ever dreamed.

> *"And these words, which I am commanding you today, shall be on your heart; and you shall teach them diligently to your sons and shall talk of them when you sit in your*

*house and when you walk by the way and when you lie down and when you rise up."*

*- Deuteronomy 6:6-7*

## Your View of Authority

If you don't believe that you have God-given authority to rule over your children for their good, you may as well close this book right now. Nothing in it will work, and then you'll blame me! No thanks, I rather you didn't read it at all. I don't care what your teachers in school told you, or what you learned from the hospital-sponsored parenting classes you took. Simply put, the Bible teaches that an understanding of authority is an essential part of parenting, and indeed an essential key to faith itself. The Scriptures tell us that it was for this very purpose that Abraham was chosen to be the father of God's chosen people. *Genesis 18:19* says, *"For I have chosen him, in order that he may command his children and his household after him to keep the way of the LORD by doing righteousness and justice; in order that the LORD may bring upon Abraham what He has spoken about him."* This is what we should be doing as we parent our children. This is a large part of what God considers good parenting.

Another of my favorite Biblical passages about authority is the story in *Matthew 8:5-13,* of the Roman centurion, who asked Jesus to heal his desperately ill servant. When Jesus offered to go to his home to do the healing, the centurion refused the offer, explaining that it was unnecessary. He knew that Jesus had authority even over sickness, and a simple word would be sufficient. Jesus marveled at this man's faith. Because this centurion understood authority, his servant was healed immediately and he himself was held up as an example of extraordinary faith to all Christians henceforth. Isn't that the kind of faith we would all someday like to see in our children?

Throughout the Old and New Testaments are stories of faith mixed with obedience, one working together closely with the other. As our Lord loves us and teaches us, He continually gives us commands and expects us to obey them. These are all very clear examples illustrating how we are to love and command our own children. In following our Lord's example, we are not only painting a picture for our children of what their relationship with God can be like someday, we are also instilling in them the type of faith that Jesus praised in this Roman centurion. Embrace the authority God has given you over your children, combine it with love and diligence, and use it for their good, to train them in the ways of Lord and lead them into eternal fellowship with Him.

> *But the centurion answered and said, "Lord, I am not worthy for You to come under my roof, but just say the word, and my servant will be healed. For I, too, am a man under authority, with soldiers under me; and I say to this one, 'Go!' and he goes, and to another, 'Come!' and he comes, and to my slave, 'Do this!' and he does it." Now when Jesus heard this, He marveled, and said to those who were following, "Truly I say to you, I have not found such great faith with anyone in Israel."*
>
> *- Matthew 8:8-10*

## Your Commitment to Godly Separation

You can do everything I recommend in this book and still lose your children to the world. How? By not separating them from wrong influences until they are very mature in their training and faith. (I believe this maturity comes far more slowly than most parents assume.) Jesus told us very clearly in *Matthew 6:24*, that *"No one can serve two masters; for either he will hate the one and love the other, or he will hold to one and despise the other...."* When you allow your children to be exposed to questionable outside influences, you are only pushing them into the arms of a second master. Considering the many exciting temptations the world has to offer, it is unlikely that their loyalty will remain with you. If you don't separate your children from the world, they may reject you and choose the ways of the world, to your own sorrow and shame.

Removing the TV and choosing to homeschool are two of the most obvious and effective solutions to the problem of wrong influences. Beyond those, one of the most enjoyable and simple things you can do to produce godly children is to keep them doing more things with you, and fewer things with other children. If you keep them with you and teach them all you know about godliness, AND you keep them away from wrong influences when they are young, you will scarcely have to worry about anything else. You will eliminate a myriad of problems that result from allowing or encouraging your children to frequently socialize with other children.

If anyone doubts how much good this can do, just read carefully the many desperate stories of Christian mothers whose children are straying, and pay strict attention to how much the matter of "outside influences" factored into the problems they are having. If you are honest in your assessment, you will find that a vast number of these problems are the direct result of the influence of "friends" outside the family. This is where your children will learn destructive secular values. This is where your children will pick up attitudes that are anti-family and anti-authority. This is where your children will be exposed to many things you never wanted them to have anything to do with. This is where they will lose their loyalty toward you and God and turn their loyalty toward the world.

If you want to raise your children to choose the Lord as their God, you must reject the world's unrelenting chant that your children "need" to socialize outside your home. Instead, you must believe the Lord when He says, *"Therefore, come out from their midst and be separate."*

> *"Therefore, come out from their midst and be separate," says the Lord. "And do not touch what is unclean; and I will welcome you. And I will be a father to you, and you shall be sons and daughters to me," says the Lord Almighty.*
>
> *- II Corinthians 6:17-18*

## Rejecting the Deception of Psychology-based Parenting

Virtually every parenting book published in recent years—both Christian and secular—was written by a psychologist, not experienced parents or grandparents. This is deeply disturbing because the field of psychology does not have its foundation in Christian principles, but vain worldly philosophies. At first these humanistic theories were only taught to those who planned to major in the field of mental health. But it wasn't long before some clever humanists in the educational world saw the opportunity to broaden their influence, and psychology became a prerequisite in nearly all college curriculums.

Courses designed specifically for future social workers and teachers are now saturated with psychology. Many careers today that deal with children require a degree in Child Psychology or Early Childhood Development. Today, beginning as early as nursery school, children are being exposed to worldly methods and techniques originally invented in failed attempts to treat the mentally ill. By the time these students reach adulthood, their viewpoints have been so shaped by secular psychology that they can scarcely think any other way. Naturally, they begin raising their own children in the same tradition, instilling in them the same ungodly values and reasoning they were taught. What better way for Satan to steal the hearts of our children away from the Lord, but to subtly slip his distortions into the belief system of young students via our schools.

Frankly, a chill runs up my spine every day as I read the many queries from young parents coming out of our modern school systems. Even though they are Christians, most don't realize what is happening as they repeat to me the worldly beliefs instilled in them by the schools. Even the churches are beginning to accept these secular philosophies, as psychologists are deemed "experts" virtually everywhere. These poor deceived parents are like the Ninevites, of whom the Lord said in *Jonah 4:11*, they *"don't know the difference between their right and left hand."*

So where do we go from here? I am reminded of the passage in Scripture concerning King Ahaziah, who had inquired of a heathen god as to whether he would recover from a serious illness. God sent Elijah the prophet to tell the king in *2 Kings 1:6*: *"Thus says the LORD, 'Is it because there is no God in Israel that you are sending to inquire of Baal-zebub, the god of Ekron? Therefore you shall not come down from the bed where you have gone up, but shall surely die.'"* It is my prayer that if you are like these parents, duped by the world's philosophies in the form of psychology, your eyes will be opened and the truth about God's way of parenting will be revealed to you through His Word, and that you will have the courage to reject the evil you have been taught. Let us begin going to the Lord for direction in all of our lives, including our parenting, and not to the world.

> *"Beloved, do not believe every spirit, but test the spirits to see whether they are from God; because many false prophets have gone out into the world."*
>
> *- I John 4:1*

Part II

# Starting With Obedience

*I am not able to go out and witness and evangelize like some people may. My mission field is my home and this houseful of children God has given to me. It is my prayer that when people see my family out in the world they will see us "shining as lights in a wicked and perverse generation" and we will be able to point them to the source of our light – Jesus.*

***Lorraine***

# two

# RAISING A GODLY CHILD

*"My son, do not forget my teaching, but let your heart keep my commandments; for length of days and years of life, and peace they will add to you. Do not let kindness and truth leave you; bind them around your neck, write them on the tablet of your heart."*

*- Proverbs 3:1-3*

## A Call for Help

*Dear Elizabeth,*

*Help. I'm completely overwhelmed. I feel as though I've been doing everything wrong. I have several young children and they are out of control and I'm totally frustrated. I want to change things, but don't know how or where to begin.*

*Sincerely,*
*Just One Desperate Mom*

Although I have answered many pleas like the one above in the recent years, when I first began recording the things I believed about childrearing, I did so primarily for my own family. I wanted to have a record of what I'd learned to pass on to my children. I felt my purpose in life was as Abraham's: *"For I have chosen him, in order that he may command his children and his household after him to keep the way of the LORD by doing righteousness and justice…." - Genesis 18:19*

We never know what the Lord has in store for us, so I wasn't positive I'd be around when my children began raising their own children. Even if I were, I don't have the best memory, so I wasn't positive I'd remember how to deal with a toddler or preschooler by then. I thought that while I was still in the trenches, I better begin writing down the basics of what I'd learned and had come to believe, and how I'd applied it all to my own children. I wanted my children to have this record to help guide them with their own children someday. After typing away in notepad for awhile (I'm not very computer savvy), I asked my oldest son, then about twenty years old, if he could set me up a website to make it easier for me to organize my sound bites of parenting knowledge.

Although I never promoted or advertised my website, word got around. Soon emails from desperate moms seeking parenting advice began consuming all my writing time, so the next step was a message board. I'd participated in several others and I thought it would be easier for me to handle questions via a forum where members could learn from each other's questions and I could address multiple parents at the same time. My message board membership quickly grew to several thousand before the sheer size of it forced me to close it to new registrations except by referral. Knowing that I could never respond to everyone who wanted help, I turned back to the task of writing down at least an overview of what the Lord had taught me about parenting, looking toward eventually turning it into a book. This time it would be aimed not just toward my own family, but toward making this information available to any mom interested in raising godly children.

*But if any of you lacks wisdom, let him ask of God, who gives to all men generously and without reproach, and it will be given to him.*

*- James 1:5*

## My Response

If I could tell this mom just one very practical thing to help her get going, it would be this: **Keep your children close to you** one hundred percent of the time. I call this Tomato Staking. I'll talk about it more later in the book, but it's really not much more than what used to be called "watching your children," with a good dose of fellowship and mentoring added to it. If you do this, you'll be able to see everything they are doing, encouraging and correcting as desired. You will get to know your children and will learn to recognize and understand what is going on inside their heads and their hearts. You cannot know and train a child who is not near enough to you to be known and trained. Keep your children with you. This will provide you with the **opportunity** to be the kind of parent you'd really like to be.

Your goal should be godly children. That means you must train their hearts to think as God thinks and their bodies to do what God would do. Keep them right with you (the younger and most untrained ones by your side, the older and better trained ones at least in the same room until they are absolutely trustworthy elsewhere). Love, nurture, encourage and educate them constantly. Teach them who God is and what His ways are like. When they disobey, or display a bad attitude, or do anything a godly child would not do, correct them promptly and require them to repeat what they did in a godly manner. Once they have obeyed you with a pleasant attitude (never proceed until they do), go back to enjoying your children as you were before. Watch your children.

*"The eyes of the LORD are in every place, watching the evil and the good."*

*- Proverbs 15:3*

## Focus on the Heart

Sadly, since starting my parenting website in 2002, I have received hundreds of Internet appeals like the one above. These parents are sincere in wanting to raise their children for the Lord, but don't know how. The psychology-based parenting methods, so popular today, are not working for them. Most have floundered for a few years, trying different failing methods, and now find themselves with rowdy young ones who do not respect them, do not obey them, and are headed toward disaster rather than faith in the living God.

It is my hope that this book will reach and help many young parents in this situation. I have focused primarily on toddlers through grade-school aged children, but have touched on older children in later chapters. I have used many of the questions I have received via email or my website message board to help explain the concepts I want to share. I have tried to give examples and suggest dialogues where I thought they would be helpful. Although teaching basic obedience is the starting point, the heart is always the real issue. Raising godly children is impossible without knowing how to reach and address their hearts; therefore I have tried to promote a focus on the heart throughout this book, over and above anything else. As you read my suggestions, do not take them as strict step-by-step rules. Instead, try to understand the principles underneath the rules, then be creative and wise as you apply them, so that they will best reach your own child's heart, turning him toward the Lord and toward you.

> *"And it shall come about, if you listen obediently to my commandments which I am commanding you today, to love the LORD your God and to serve Him with all your heart and all your soul..."*
>
> *- Deuteronomy 11:13*

# three

# THE BASICS AND BEFORE

*"For I, too, am a man under authority,*
*with soldiers under me; and I say to this*
*one, 'Go!' and he goes, and to another,*
*'Come!' and he comes..."*
*- Matthew 8:9*

## Teaching Obedience So You Don't Have to Teach Anything Else

In our home, we begin training our children to conform to the image of God when they are still small by teaching only one thing: that they must always obey us with a willing and pleasant spirit. When we start with just that one thing, we don't have to do much else. What could be more simple? Once your child understands obedience, everything else is pretty much taken care of. Henceforth, you can simply ask him to come to you and he will. You can ask him to pick up his toys and he will. You can ask him to get ready for bed and he will trot off and do so. You can even ask him to "stop crying," and he will stop. Simple. Obedience is really all you need to teach a little one.

Yes, maintenance work upon on occasion will be necessary, and you will still have to do much teaching and guiding, but do you see the potential? Once you've convinced your child that his rightful duty is to obey his parents, the need for discipline will virtually disappear. You won't be correcting your child every few minutes as you might envision, but only very rarely, and usually a simple verbal rebuke will be enough. Since the big Parent vs. Child power struggle will be over, you will be able to spend the vast majority of your time enjoying your child the way you've always hoped to, teaching the things that are important to you and sharing the things you both find interesting. This is the way parenting was intended to be.

*The conclusion, when all has been heard, is: fear God and keep His commandments, because this applies to every person.*
*- Ecclesiastes 12:13-14*

## What First?

**Laura:** Okay, I've thrown out all my popular feel-good parenting books and I'm ready to begin all over. What should I train for first? My child doesn't come when he's called, can't sit still in church, constantly touches things he should not, and I just don't know how to handle his awful temper tantrums. Where do I start and what do I do?

**Elizabeth:** There really is no order, just a starting date. Remember that you are not teaching a series of tasks, but obedience in general. Pick a date and commit yourself to keeping your child near you and training diligently from that moment onward. Enjoy your child and encourage him in all he does well and right. Correct him every time he resists obeying you. Then keep it up.

There. That ought to do it.

Okay, okay, I'll elaborate. For example, if your day is moving along smoothly, then suddenly your toddler refuses to come when you call him, stop what you are doing and take the time to train him to do as you asked and come to you. Don't allow him to do anything else until he obeys you. Don't back down or give up until he comes to you willingly and quickly about three times in a row. Then, once he is again obeying you nicely, let him go back to playing. Or better yet, spend some time teaching and enjoying him.

If, fifteen minutes later, you ask him to give back the toy he just grabbed from his brother, and he refuses and begins whining, stop what you are doing, take up the challenge and see that he does what you asked him to. Then require him to do it over again until he does it without whining. And so on. Correct and train him as each and every new difficulty arises. Spank if needed, reward with approval and affection when he is obeying well. Remember that your child's heart attitude is more important than his physical actions, so don't overlook pouting, whining, and other displays of a rebellious spirit. Treat those things just as you would any other wrong behavior. It is simply a wrong behavior of the heart.

It doesn't matter what you train for first. You are training your child to obey you agreeably, as he should. You are not training him to come, or to hand over a toy, or to sit still on your lap, or to do or not do any other individual task. You are training for obedience, and **if you train for obedience, you won't have to train for anything else.**

As far as tantrums go, any conflict over anything can, and likely will, turn into a tantrum if you suddenly begin insisting your untrained child obey you. That's GREAT! That's WONDERFUL! These other things are usually just small battles, whereas a tantrum is closer to a full-scale war. Would you rather win a few little battles or the whole war? Look forward to the tantrums and other major displays of stubbornness and willfulness as opportunities to win a whole war. If you win a few tantrum wars (and you must), the little skirmishes will just disappear, and so will the tantrums.

*"Children, obey your parents in the Lord, for this is right."*
*- Ephesians 6:1*

## Before You Discipline

Now I can hear my readers saying, "That was too simple, too general, too much of a condensed version. How do we really do it? Give us details. Give us a list. Tell us where exactly to begin. HOW do I teach my toddler to obey me?" All right, I will get to specifics and examples in the next chapter, but first I want to cover some important areas that need to be pondered *before* you begin training and kept in mind *all the while* you are training. These things apply to children of all ages, and actually become more important the older your children become.

Some are specifics, like asking yourself a few discerning questions before you discipline, and speaking softly and being consistent, while others are generalities such as how to encourage your child with the proper type and amount of praise, and how to overcome parental anger aroused by childish behavior. After we cover these preparatory issues, I will give a very brief, seven-step "how to" plan for toddler training, then continue forward in the following chapter with plenty of details and examples to help you along.

*How blessed is the man who finds wisdom, and the man who gains understanding.*
*- Proverbs 3:13*

## When to Discipline

Although most of us tend to expect too little of our children rather than too much, we should still ask ourselves some questions before disciplining, in order to eliminate any possibility of disciplining unjustly, as warned against in *Ephesians 6:4*. Did my child understand me? Is he capable of doing what I asked? Is there some underlying problem that needs correcting first? Am I being consistent? Am I looking at actions only, or at my child's heart and working to correct what is inside? Am I correcting because I am angry, or because I truly want what is best for my child? Such questions, asked before disciplining, will enable you to know when to discipline, and when to overlook childish errors. When you do discipline, they will help you determine the best type of correction for each child in each particular situation. Never discipline according to a fixed list of rules without regard to special or unique circumstances. Use your God-given common sense to apply discipline with justice and mercy.

> *"...For I knew that Thou art a gracious and compassionate God, slow to anger and abundant in lovingkindness, and one who relents concerning calamity."*
>
> *- Jonah 4:2*

## No Yelling Allowed

When you correct your child, do not raise your voice. We've all heard parents who call, "Bobby? Bob... BOB... ROBERT! COME HERE RIGHT NOW!" When you do it that way, all you are doing is training your child *not* to obey you *until* you raise your voice. He knows you won't do anything about his disobedience until then, so why should he bother to obey prior to the last second? Don't do it like that. Pause before you direct, and think about how you'd really like to be able to instruct your child and still get a cooperative prompt response. Wouldn't you like to be able to just use your regular voice? To just ask politely one time and get a positive, willing reply? Then train your child with that in mind. Call and instruct him in your regular voice. Do not call him twice if you know he heard you the first time. Get up and correct him if he doesn't respond promptly and correctly to your first call. Be firm with your voice if necessary, but always be as consistently calm and pleasant as possible. Paul M. Landis, in *The Responsibility of Parents in Teaching and Training Their Children* says, *"Consistency with gentleness, a quiet manner and voice, and firmness, rather than anger with a loud, high-pitched voice, will convince a child of our sincerity and purpose."* I couldn't agree more.

> *By forbearance a ruler may be persuaded, and a soft tongue breaks the bone.*
>
> *- Proverbs 25:15*

## Consistency

The degree of success you achieve will be directly related to how consistent you are. Don't get lazy. Don't give up. Don't make excuses. Don't be "on again, off again" about training your children. Keep your children with you and watch them, correcting all disobedience and bad attitudes. Say what you mean and mean what you say. Don't be afraid to set high standards and maintain them. Teach and train your children, then expect them to act in a godly manner. Require them to always act the way *you* would like them to act, and the way you believe God would like them to act, not the way others may let their children act. Be consistent in your training and in your expectations.

Consistency does not mean "do exactly the same thing with every child" or "discipline the same exact way in every instant." Not every child has the same personality or emotional makeup. Not every circumstance is the same. The age of the child will factor in. Some children are more strong-willed and stubborn than others. A child's motivation will vary from time to time and incident to incident. Some children have been in the habit of rebellion longer than others. These and other things must be taken into consideration as you determine how to handle each child and situation, but this should not interfere with true consistency. **Consistency really means that every time your child requires correction, you get up and do it, remaining there to supervise and outlast until the message gets across.** Instead of trying to handle each child and event uniformly, try to envision the end result you want, and then adjust your methods to get each child there in each situation. Strive to be "consistent" about correcting each and every time it is needed.

> *He who spares his rod hates his son, but he who loves him disciplines him diligently.*
>
> *- Proverbs 13:24*

## My Change to Consistency

I remember a specific day years ago when my oldest three children were still young. I was talking to a friend on the phone, and I remember telling the caller that I could hear my little daughter jumping on the couch in the other room, and that I "really should go stop her...." Then it hit me. Yes, that's exactly what I needed to do in order to begin seeing some lasting results in my efforts to raise godly children. I needed to stop talking to my friends on the phone, and go correct my daughter every single time she needed it. That would be true consistency, and I hadn't been doing it.

So, I decided to change. I resolved to make consistency my top priority. I stopped running unnecessary errands, stopped over-indulging in my hobbies, stopped making excessive social phone calls, and set my mind diligently and consistently on training my children. I continued with the normal mandatory tasks of life, such as basic housekeeping, laundry, and cooking, but even as I did those things, I kept in mind that my children were my *top* priority, not a fancy dinner or a spotless house. I gathered my children close to me so I could always see and hear them, then I stopped what I was doing and promptly corrected them, *every time* they needed it.

At first, numerous corrections were necessary and I had my doubts about the strategy, but very soon there was noticeable improvement in the way they responded to me. The worst was over after only a few days, and hardly any major disciplining was needed after the first few weeks. By the end of the third month, I had a new family. They had, in just that short amount of time, acquired a whole new respect for me and for my words. It was a miracle, produced mostly the simple consistency that God instructs us to use!

> *Therefore, my beloved brethren, be steadfast, immovable, always abounding in the work of the Lord, knowing that your toil is not in vain in the Lord.*
>
> \- *I Corinthians 15:58*

## Not Always Disciplining

If you find yourself perpetually disciplining, it is likely that you are not watching your child. If you are not watching your child you cannot be truly consistent. If you correct a child ten times and then skip once, you will have undone everything you accomplished on the last ten occasions. Now, if you correct diligently *one hundred times* and then overlook some minor transgression, it won't take long to reestablish order, but remember: you must be consistent one hundred times in a row *first*. Are you doing this?

Now I don't mean you should have to correct your child a hundred times for the same thing. That's not it at all. Just one hundred times for any disobedience of any kind—IN A ROW. You have to convince your child that he must *always* obey you before you can overlook an occasional infraction without it resulting in a major behavioral relapse. By then, it is very likely that you will have trained his conscience to the point where it will admonish him even if you don't.

> *Create in me a clean heart, O God, and renew a steadfast spirit within me.*
>
> \- *Psalms 51:10*

## Love in Parenting

When I first began writing about child rearing, I focused mostly on discipline because so many parents were failing in that area. They loved their children, but didn't know how to discipline them.

Then I began receiving criticism for "never writing about loving your children". What?

As I reflected on this complaint, I realized that I had assumed that loving and enjoying children was a simple, natural phenomenon commonly understood and universally practiced by all parents. I didn't think I *needed* to write about it! Wrong. I found that there are indeed well-intentioned parents who go overboard with discipline, standards, and structure, but are wholly ignorant about how to express love to their children. With that in mind, I began including advice on this most mandatory part of successful child rearing: loving your child.

If your children are models of perfect behavior, but starved for love, they will eventually turn from you and probably from God as well. Don't let that happen. Learn to love, and express that love, to your children. Build a relationship with them of the sort that will encourage them to want to obey you and eventually the Lord. Keeping your children close to you via Tomato Staking will make this possible.

> *Remember, O LORD, Thy compassion and Thy lovingkindness, for they have been from of old.*
>
> *- Psalms 25:6*

## Tomato Staking With Love

Besides making it possible to watch and correct your children, Tomato Staking makes it possible to nurture your children with love. Keep your children with you. Hug, kiss, sing, laugh and play with them. Include them in the things you are doing. Smile at them when they come to you to show you something. Welcome their attention. Answer their questions. Invite them into your lap for a cuddle. Let them crawl into your bed and snuggle up to you now and then. When they ask to help you, say, "Sure." Joke and laugh with them. Share with them your sense of humor. Be interested in the things they are interested in and be excited about their accomplishments as you tutor them in all of God's ways. Get to know them and let them get to know you. Can a child who is the constant recipient of such joyful companionship ever doubt that he is deeply and profoundly loved? I don't think so.

I know that all moms are beset with endless chores and duties, but these should never take precedence over your children. If you are Tomato Staking with an abundance of love, you will soon find that discipline consumes a progressively diminishing portion of your time, freeing you up for those chores. So, especially when you are first starting out, set aside what tasks you can, and address your child's needs for both discipline and love, whenever they arise.

*Draw near to God and He will draw near to you.*

*- James 4:8*

## Guarding Your Child's Trust

If you love your children, you will discipline them when needed. But when you discipline, you must do so justly and without anger. The Bible says not to *"provoke your children to wrath."* We must be certain that we are just in the way we treat our children. The following checklist of questions will help you determine if your discipline is appropriate and just, or whether you are at risk of provoking your children to wrath.

Do you betray your child's trust and confidence by ignoring an infraction one day, then punishing for the same infraction the next? Or do you consistently watch and correct them whenever needed?

Do you emotionally unsettle your children by praising them one minute, then yelling at them the next? Or do you control your own emotions and consistently address them with calmness and peace?

Do you constantly pick on your children for trivial transgressions? Or do you consistently show love and affection the majority of the time?

Do you spring unreasonable demands on your children without warning? Or do you let them know clearly what is expected of them ahead of time if at all possible?

Do you discipline them just as severely for a simple accident as you do for outright defiance, or are you appropriately merciful when an innocent mistake occurs?

Are you unreasonably regimented for no good reason? Or are you flexible and understanding when possible?

Are you always suspicious or your children's motives, conveying it by constant accusations and criticisms? Or do you trust your children when they've earned your trust, and let them know it by your words, smiles and the privileges you allow them?

Do you emotionally abuse your children with unnecessary shaming, belittling, and manipulation? Or are you reasonable, straightforward and direct when dealing with them?

Do you leave your children feeling that no matter how hard they try, they can never quite measure up anyway? Or do they know they will receive your approval as long as they make a sincere effort to do what is right?

Are you a critical, controlling ogre? Or are you the pleasant, loving parent you ought to be?

How you treat your children in all of these things will profoundly determine the quality of your relationship with them. One thing is absolutely certain: a good relationship will lay a foundation for the growth of true Christian character in our children, and of a close relationship between them and God Himself in the future. A poor parent/child relationship will almost certainly frustrate and undermine the development of the godliness that is the goal of our sacred labors. An unjust, unkind and unreasonable parent can easily lead our children to reject the Lord completely in the end. Please take this to heart and build a close, loving relationship with your child that models the relationship our Lord offers us.

*And, fathers, do not provoke your children to anger; but bring them up in the discipline and instruction of the Lord.*
*- Ephesians 6:4*

## The Essential Element of Praise

*Reasonable* praise is an important part of the way in which parents should be expressing love for their children. Tragically, I have met parents who never praise their children. Rather, they constantly find fault and criticize. I know other parents who praise generously, but do it the wrong way or at the wrong time. Some are so worried about building self-esteem that they praise excessively, creating pride and false confidence instead. So let's consider for a moment, some of the right ways and wrong ways to praise a child.

Be free with your praise without lavishing your child with undeserved flattery. Avoid offering praise for things he had nothing to do with, such as physical attributes, looks, or in-born intelligence. Don't encourage your child to take praise for granted by offering it for every trifle. Be generous with sincere and modest praise when it is warranted. Be particularly attentive to extending it for overcoming a temptation, making a good effort, or for "going the extra mile" in doing what is right. Encourage your child to be of godly character and consistently give him your warm approval when he demonstrates such. That is the best kind of praise.

> *His master said to him, 'Well done, good and faithful slave; you were faithful with a few things, I will put you in charge of many things, enter into the joy of your master.'*
> *- Matthew 25:21*

## Praise after Defiance

I never praise a child for obeying me after having initially defied me. For example, if I tell my little boy to go get a spoon for me and he cheerfully obeys, I usually say with a smile, "Thank you!" That simple smile and thank you shows approval and is all the praise a small child wants or needs. Sometimes I will compliment his attitude also, saying, "Thank you! I like your happy smile when I ask you to do something." This is even better praise and will encourage your child to continue to do well and seek to please you.

However, if a request is performed grudgingly and reluctantly, the first thing I do is correct my child's bad attitude: "Now, go back and do that again—with a smile this time." Then, when he obeys the way he should have initially, I will say matter-of-factly, "Good. That's much better." I might also add, "Now remember to do it that way the *first* time I ask you." Sometimes I'll smile and say, "Good. It's so much nicer when you obey with a willing smile." In these types of situations I am not praising, just directing, and indicating acceptance of his ultimate obedience. I always make sure my child knows I approve of his belated obedience, but I never hypocritically offer excessive praise after he's just tested or defied me. It is much wiser to instill in him the unmistakable impression that his initial rebellion was a serious offense not to be repeated. Genuine praise should be earned.

> *And a voice came out of the heavens: "Thou art My beloved Son, in Thee I am well-pleased."*
> *- Mark 1:11*

## Attitude of Approval

The most important part of a good praise strategy is not the specific words or the timing, but how your overall attitude reflects perpetual loving approval and encouragement. Look carefully into your children's ways, and express with your countenance, words, and actions that you are pleased with them for the good that you see. When you assess your children, scrutinize their hearts and motives, not just their outward actions. Be particularly alert to expressions of kindness, generosity, hard work, positive attitudes, and other indications of good character. Be especially quick to praise your child when he makes a difficult choice to do the right thing. Let him know that not only do *you* approve of him, but so does God.

Praise of the most effective kind may be communicated without the use of words. Simply letting your children know that you are pleased with them is effective praise—the best kind really—and should be done frequently. Overall, your children should always feel they are covered by your love and approval, just as we, the sheep of our Lord's flock, know for a certainty that we are the objects of His unconditional love and acceptance.

> *Pleasant words are a honeycomb, sweet to the soul and healing to the bones.*
>
> *- Proverbs 16:24*

## Parental Anger Related to Childrearing

Most of us can relate to feeling frustrated and angry with our children from time to time. Parental anger and frustration are usually the result of one of two things: ignorance of effective parenting strategies or wrong parental priorities. A parent who does not know how to handle an out-of-control child will certainly become frustrated, and this frustration will often turn to anger. On the other hand, if you know exactly what to do when your child begins to misbehave, and you are willing to do it, you will simply handle the matter and move on. Stress will be eliminated and replaced with a feeling of satisfaction with a parenting job well done.

Sometimes parents know what to do, but are simply unwilling to do it. They expect their children to behave perfectly with little or no effort on their part. Or they expect their children to just stay out of the way while they proceed with their lives as if their children didn't exist. They let their ambitions, housework, or hobbies become a higher priority than parenting, and they begin to view their children as annoying interruptions. This attitude guarantees failure, frustration, and anger. Only by reordering priorities and recognizing that parenting is a highly demanding, full time job will there be any hope for decent results and the absence of frustration. Give up everything else if necessary, and undertake the world's most important and fulfilling job to the best of your ability. Expect it to be a demanding job at times, but look forward to the challenge instead of resenting it. Parenting will be far less frustrating if you learn how to do it well, and if it is not competing with everything else for your time and attention.

> *And so, as those who have been chosen of God, holy and beloved, put on a heart of compassion, kindness, humility, gentleness and patience…*
>
> *- Colossians 3:12*

## 7 Quick Steps to Toddler Obedience

Okay, now that you've pondered some underlying principles and prepared yourself for the task of parenting, here's the stripped-down, shortcut method for teaching toddler obedience.

If you have a toddler who is old enough to understand you, and who is capable of following your instructions, you can and should teach him to obey. In almost every case, the following general steps are all it takes:

1. Watch your child and notice when he is doing something you disapprove of. Each time this happens, stop what you are doing and call him over to you. Make EYE CONTACT.

2. Tell him clearly what you expect him to do or not to do. SAY WHAT YOU MEAN.

3. WATCH to see that your instructions are carried out.

4. Correct him upon the FIRST refusal to obey. Do this with some immediate, negative consequence like a firm "No" or a small swat on the bottom. MEAN WHAT YOU SAY.

5. Direct your child to repeat what you asked him to do, correctly this time.

6. Repeat all of the above as many times as it takes, until the child obeys with a good attitude—one of cooperativeness and willingness to obey. OUTLAST him. This is mandatory.

7. Keep your child with you and watch him diligently, correcting every future misbehavior of any kind, in similar fashion. Be CONSISTENT.

Now those are the bare bones basics. I'm going to tell you many more things to help you along the way, but if you keep your toddler with you and follow these few short steps each time there is a conflict, you'll be well on your way to success in no time. Always remember to encourage and enjoy your child whenever he is responding well to you and living as a godly child should.

*But above all, my brethren…let your yes be yes, and your no, no….*

*- James 5:12*

# four

# STARTING EARLY

*Discipline your son while there is hope.*
*- Proverbs 19:18*

## Starting Early: The Rationale

Starting early means teaching your child to obey you as soon as he is able to understand the word "no." That is usually well before he is a year old. I begin the training process about the time my little ones begin to crawl. At first, it's more of a preparatory phase, where I teach them what "no" means, and check extremes of willfulness or temper. Later, when I expect more of them, I have a much easier time of it. They've already learned that they can't do whatever they please, that Dad and I are their rightful authorities in life, and that they must obey us. This makes all later training dramatically easier.

Childrearing is not only easier on you, when begun early, but on your child as well. Is it really a kindness to give your child complete freedom to be selfish, willful, and self-centered, then suddenly, a few years later, to change up on him and expect him to be respectful, considerate, and self-controlled? It seems to me to be both kinder and wiser to teach good character from the outset. No big shock to the system. Your child won't feel betrayed because you've changed the rules on him. He'll have more confidence and more trust in you, because he's known from the beginning what expectations and limits are in place.

The heart of a young child is more innocently naive to sin than that of an older child who has succeeded for some time in using wrong behavior for selfish goals. Very young children may be self-centered, but this natural self-centeredness has not yet escalated into scheming, haughtiness, and other more sophisticated character flaws. Because the young are less complex, and still unconfirmed in their willfulness, they are easier to persuade and shape. And this process of shaping is enjoyable to them, not stressful. They are also more transparent and honest at younger ages and so have far more difficulty obscuring wrong thoughts and inclinations. This makes it easier for you to understand them and teach them. And young children are more focused on you. They need you more, want you more, and are therefore easier to motivate with both praise and discipline.

If you start early, you are not tempting your child to sin by overlooking character flaws. Every wrong, destructive character quality is just as damaging in a two-year-old as it is in a twenty-two-year-old and just as easily encouraged by the neglect of discipline. Selfishness in a two-year-old is just as wrong as selfishness in a ten-year-old, so if you allow your two-year-old to be selfish, you are just allowing him to sin. If you continue to allow selfishness, you will be encouraging a *pattern* of sinning in his life, tempting him to sin still further as he learns that there will be no repercussions.

Although I strongly promote early child training, there is no reason to go to extremes and attempt to train tiny babies only a few months old. Enjoy your wee ones, but don't delay discipline and training forever. It's perilous to wait until your child has reached the hefty age of two or three years old, as many of the so-called childrearing experts of today are now recommending. If you do, you will surely have the dubious pleasure of experiencing the "terrible twos (or threes)" in full force. Don't assume that because you didn't teach them anything up until they were preschoolers, they weren't learning anything on their own. Children are always learning, and what they are learning when you are putting off child training, is that they can be as self-centered and self-willed as they please. If this is what they have learned by default, realize that you will have a much harder time turning them around when you finally get fed up with it.

*...a child who gets his own way brings shame to his mother.*
*- Proverbs 29:15*

## Teaching "No"

Normal healthy babies are all capable of understanding "no" by the time they can crawl, and often well before that. For a little while, I just move them away from temptations or distract them to avoid trouble, but eventually (the sooner, the better—at least before the age of one) I get serious about teaching them to obey, and use the word "no" to do it.

I start by firmly telling them "No" when they reach for something they shouldn't, then stopping them a few times to get the idea across. The next step is to require them to actually obey me when I say "No," rather than removing or stopping them myself. I watch for them to reach for something they have been told is forbidden. I tell them "No," and if they continue to reach for the object, I give them a mild swat on their diapered bottom and say "No" again, but I don't remove them or physically stop them unless necessary.

These little ones are usually puzzled and try to reach for the object a couple of more times, receiving a definite "No" accompanied by a mild, but decided, swat each time. Most of my babies got the idea after just a few "no's" and accompanying firm pats on the bottom. They either turned and crawled away, or sat and cried for a minute until I redirected them to something else. Sometimes they pouted briefly in disappointment, then turned to something else on their own. Once I can see that they are resigned to submission, I congratulate them and then point toward something else, if needed, and encourage them to go play. It is important to let them know what to do, not just what not to do.

> *And all these blessings shall come upon you and overtake you,*
> *if you will obey the LORD your God.*
> *- Deuteronomy 28:2*

## From Then On

From that time forward, I always make them obey any direction I give. I stop distracting them and removing them from temptations. I stop giving repeated warnings. I make clear what I want, and teach them to obey. Don't think of this as discipline. Think of it as training. You can start training very early—as soon as your baby is old enough to be taught what you mean by "No, no."

> *...the precious possession of a man is diligence.*
> *- Proverbs 12:27*

## A Word about Little Hands

By the way, never swat little hands. Little hands are delicate things, and easily injured. God provides a better place—one that is well padded. If my baby is heading with determination for the electrical outlet, I don't wait until he gets there, then swat his hand as he reaches for it. Instead, I stop him *before* he getting too close for safety. Then I speak a serious, "No," and tap him on his bottom, not his hand.

Babies are surprisingly smart. They will very quickly make the connection between your pat on the bottom and your displeasure at what they are doing. In fact, in my experience, swatting a hand often suggests to them that you are playing some kind of game, not seriously saying, "No." They focus on their hand and not your words. What you want them to focus on is your word and its meaning.

The mild pat on the bottom is just a "pay attention, I'm talking to you" swat. It shouldn't be hard, just one that has a persistent air to it. Neither should you yell your "NO!" Just use a quiet, firm tone of voice and accompany it with a gentle, but firm tap on the diaper. Repeat, with reasonable pauses, until your baby listens. Do not let him do anything else until he obeys.

> *You, however, continue in the things you have learned and become convinced of...*
>
> *- II Timothy 3:14-15*

## Watch Your Baby

Watch your baby closely. You can't train him if you don't see what he is doing. If you try to correct him after the fact, he won't understand. Watch him and correct him *as* he disobeys. Babies have surprisingly good memories, but don't expect him to have a perfect memory. Just repeat the same process again, if he forgets or tries to test you. Your training will be useless if you say "no" to something and then do nothing a few minutes later when he repeats the same offense. Be careful not to give too many commands and directions at first, but when you do tell him something, always make certain he obeys. Watch him and be ready to correct him as soon as he disobeys you the next time and every time thereafter.

> *For the ways of a man are before the eyes of the LORD, and He watches all his paths.*
>
> *- Proverbs 5:21*

## What a Little One is Capable of Learning

Some parents expect too much from their children, but generally, most parents do not expect enough. A one-year-old can be taught to sit quietly in church, for example, and to remain seated at a restaurant and even to be quiet when his mom tells him to.

Most things will require repetition. Be consistent and you'll be surprised at how much the littlest ones can understand and how well-behaved they can be. After teaching your child the meaning of the word "no" and to obey you when you use it, you can apply that word to all of the following and more, according to the child's ability and understanding. Practice some of these things during dinner or story time. Picture a well-behaved, happy little one, then teach your child to act that way. I'm going to give some specific examples and directions here, but don't limit yourself to just those I mention. Look for anything your child can be taught to understand, such as holding still for a diaper change, staying where you tell him to stay, not touching forbidden objects, looking at you when you call his name, and so on. You can expect him to obey you in all of these things and more.

*Correct your son, and he will give you comfort; he will also delight your soul.*

*- Proverbs 29:17*

## "Put Your Head Down"

It is helpful to teach a baby to put his head down on your shoulder when you tell him to do so. Just wait for the appropriate opportunity (when you have time to just stand and hold him, and possibly when he is sleepy) and push the side of his head gently down on your shoulder. When he picks it up, say, "No. Put your head down," and gently push his head down again. Repeat until he keeps his head down. Expect this to take a while, but eventually he will learn what you mean, and to obey you.

*Take hold of instruction; do not let go. Guard her, for she is your life.*

*- Proverbs 4:1*

## Infant Temper Tantrums

Some children possess strong tempers even when they are very young. If your baby stiffens and throws a full-fledged screaming fit of anger when there is nothing wrong except that he isn't getting his way, hold him tightly and keep telling him "no" firmly until he relaxes and submits to you. Don't relent until he does. Don't get angry; just outlast him. Once he's stopped, reward him by rocking, singing, or something else that he likes, but don't give in until he obeys you without resisting.

*A fool always loses his temper, but a wise man holds it back.*
*- Proverbs 29:11*

## Squirming

Another very good beginning lesson in obedience is teaching your baby to sit contentedly on your lap. You can begin at six months of age or even younger. My sixth baby was eleven months old when I wrote the first draft of this chapter and he had already known how to sit quietly for some weeks.

Place your baby (after he has been fed and changed) on your lap, facing away from you. When he tries to arch his back or roll over, push his tummy back down and tell him "No." Do not *hold* him down. (But don't let him fall on the floor either!)

Do this when you have time to keep it up until he stops resisting you. Outlast him. Usually a baby will cry a little bit before giving in, so expect that. *Be consistent.* Once you start this, do the same thing every time he struggles on your lap. Be sure he sits there quietly for a little while before you allow him to do something else. Be sure that YOU are the one making the decisions, not him.

*My son, do not reject the discipline of the LORD, or loathe His reproof, For whom the LORD loves He reproves, even as a father, the son in whom he delights.*

*- Proverbs 3:11-12*

## Pushing Away From You

When training little ones, look for points of resistance, then teach them to submit instead. It's common for a baby to want to be picked up, but then to immediately start twisting and turning until you feel like you're in a wrestling match, trying to prevent a fall to the floor. You need not endure that. Use it as another opportunity to teach obedience.

Squirming reflects the realization that his world is bigger than boring old Mom, and he's figured out how to use Mom as his transportation to the rest of the world. Let him look at and explore many things, but teach him limits as you do, drawing the line at him resisting you and causing you to struggle. He should look without pushing and twisting and trying to get you to go where *he* wants.

It's quite easy to do this. Just say, "No, stop that," as soon as the squirming begins, and administer a little pat on the bottom as he pushes away from you. Show by your demeanor that you disapprove. Pull him back toward you and release. Don't hold him still; require him to obey you and choose to stop struggling on his own.

Don't assume he can't understand, just because he can't talk. A puppy can't talk either, yet we all know how to communicate with a puppy. Ability to talk is not the same as ability to understand. Watch your baby's reactions to see if he understands, being certain to discern the difference between what he understands and what he is willing to do. If there is any hint that he knows what you want, he probably does. Once you know your baby understands you, just keep insisting he obey until he does.

*Listen to your father who begot you, and do not despise your mother when she is old.*

*- Proverbs 23:22*

## Refusing to Come

Most of the previous early training examples won't require much time. If you start early, little ones will usually not hold out for long. Within a few minutes, usually less than fifteen, they will give in and obey you. If sessions are repeated every time they are needed, they will soon become shorter and less frequent, until you are having no standoffs at all. Although most children learn very quickly, there are, nevertheless, some who can be quite stubborn. They will hold out a lot longer, and when they do, you must simply outlast them, no matter how long it takes.

Let me share my experience with my third-born. I waited a little too long before insisting that he always obey me, and he was two years old at the time we began training him seriously. He was well behaved compared to many two-year-olds, but had finally realized just how much he was in control of us, rather than we of him. He quickly became stubborn, willful, and prone to throwing fits. One day we were visiting some close friends and he decided to exert his newfound power. He blatantly refused to come to Dad when Dad called him. He ignored Dad and continued playing with our friend's telephone instead, about six feet from where my husband and I were sitting.

The friends we were visiting were excellent parents and offered their advice, which we readily accepted. They coached us to outlast him, instructing Dad to keep calling him. When he didn't budge, Dad was directed to go over to him, administer a little swat on the bottom (over clothes and a diaper), then return to where he'd been sitting and call him again. We were encouraged to repeat this, pausing appropriately between repeats, until he obeyed us. We never guided him back to us. We never raised our voices or let our tempers flare. We never "forced" him to obey. Sometimes we gave him a mild, but firm swat, and sometimes we only made him look at us while firmly repeating what we wanted.

Finally, after approximately an hour and a half, he began to cry and take a few steps toward us, but he still refused to come all the way. He still did not want to totally give up the power he had enjoyed exerting over us. Each time he took a few steps toward us then stopped, we would replace him back by the phone and call him to come to us again. We devoted the next half hour to making sure he obeyed completely, not just partially. When it was over, he was content and happy and ready to obey any request, just as we asked.

This one outlasting session had a considerable and exciting long-term impact on our child. He clearly learned he was under our authority and must always obey us. He only resisted obeying a few times in the following couple of weeks—a huge improvement compared to his usual previous behavior—and each time it took only about fifteen minutes to outlast him. The initial two-hour ordeal never needed repeating. It has been over twenty years since this incident and all twenty years have been extremely enjoyable with this child. I would highly recommend you adopt this method of teaching "come here" to your child if needed.

*My son, give attention to my words; incline your ear to my sayings.*

*- Proverbs 4:20*

## Too Many Tears

This question from one of my Internet message board moms focuses on a child's use of tears to gain his will:

**Bettina:** My one year old daughter understands the word "No." Occasionally when she doesn't obey promptly, I go to her, interrupt the offending activity, and firmly say, "No." Typically she will look at me, burst into a fake cry, and stop. Sometimes she'll let out a wail, then come and put her head on my leg. When she comes to me like that, I pick her up and tell her why I said "No," even though she may not completely understand what I'm saying. Am I doing this right? Am I doing enough? Should I be doing anything else?

**Elizabeth:** If she stops when you say, "No," you are doing fine. Nothing else is required. Her quick, ready compliance suggests she will likely be an easy child to raise. Continue to be alert to similar opportunities to do a little training. Don't overlook occasional disobedience just because she usually obeys so well. Also, be careful not to overdo the sympathy when she cries. You can pick her up or give a little hug and add kind words, but do not allow her to milk the situation. Too much sympathy will send the message that you can be manipulated with tears, and she will begin doing it with great regularity.

*He who pursues righteousness and loyalty finds life, righteousness and honor.*

*- Proverbs 21:21*

## Making it Stick

After attempting to follow my early obedience instructions, moms frequently complain to me that the training doesn't seem to be lasting. They have to do it over and over again. Here's an example, along with my answer:

**Calandra:** I can tell my crawler "no" when she reaches for my plants, and she will stop and crawl away from them, but the minute I turn my back or step out of the room, she's back trying to touch them again. Does she understand what I mean? When is this training going to *stick*?

**Elizabeth:** Since she goes for the plant only when you are not looking, I'd say she understands exactly what you mean—that the plant is off limits. The way you described her reaction to your "no," suggests you have trained her well so far. She clearly knows she must submit to you. Although she's learned she must obey when you are present, she still believes she can get away with disobeying when you are not right there watching. God gave little ones lots of natural curiosity and determination of spirit and they will indeed test you over and over again. That's what babies do. Eventually, if you persevere in catching her in the act and correcting her, she will understand that she must obey, whether you are around or not.

A little "ambushing" is usually very helpful in getting the message across: that she must obey you even when she can't see you. Try this: leave her in a tempting situation (perhaps near the plant), then let her think you are away (go around the corner or someplace close by, but where she can't see you). Watch her closely without her being aware. If she crawls toward the plant, wait until she decides to try to touch it, and be there to give her a sharp "No!" possibly accompanied by a little surprise swat on the bottom, just as she reaches for it.

Surprise is the key. It's the startle factor that provides that little bit of extra motivation needed to make a rule "stick" in your child's mind. A little ambushing teaches her two things—that Mom is most likely watching even when she doesn't seem to be, and that a child must always obey, whether or not she can see mom. If you are having "sticking" problems, be alert for opportunities to "ambush." Remember this: **Watch, Ambush, Repeat!**

> *My son, observe the commandment of your father, and do not forsake the teaching of your mother; bind them continually on your heart; tie them around your neck. When you walk about, they will guide you; when you sleep, they will watch over you; and when you awake, they will talk to you.*
>
> *- Proverbs 6:20-22*

## Don't Go Overboard

CAUTION! Don't go overboard and start training your six-month-old all day long as though he were in boot camp. ENJOY your babies. It's not going to hurt them to be cuddled when they cry. They don't *have* to be on a strict schedule unless that's what works best for both of you. They don't have to be saying, "Yes Ma'am," and saluting you, when they can't even crawl! If you decide to start training them early, a decision I highly recommend, focus only on simple obedience, and keep the things you ask of them age appropriate.

*Grandchildren are the crown of old men, and the glory of sons is their fathers.*

*- Proverbs 17:6*

# five

# STARTING LATER

*When I was a son to my father, tender and the only son in the sight of my mother, then he taught me and said to me, "Let your heart hold fast my words; keep my commandments and live."*

- *Proverbs 4:3-4*

## Is It Too Late to Begin Now?

Not knowing any better, I didn't start early with my three oldest children. Despite some good instincts, I had nothing to give me further direction or confidence. As the second youngest in my family, I had missed the opportunity to watch the training of my siblings. Growing up, I rarely baby-sat and wasn't around little children very often, so when I had my own children, I was clueless about raising them. I did read some popular Christian parenting books, but didn't find them very helpful, particularly with younger children. Most of them seemed to be aimed at children who were already school-aged and presumably capable of being "reasoned" with. So I struggled along in frustration for the first several years. Only when my first three children were about two, four, and six, did I commence parenting the way I do now. By those ages the "starting early" window of opportunity has passed. By age two, you are "starting later."

The training involved in starting later is not all that different from that employed in starting early, except that by this age your child will need a lot more convincing before he gives up the ruling power he's been allowed since birth. The same techniques of consistency, outlasting, ambushing, and so on can be used with these older children, but the parents will have to be a lot more diligent in applying them. Rather than starting from scratch with an unspoiled child, you will have to go through a challenging period of turning your child around. The good news is that it is still possible to do, and can often be done in a relatively short period of time.

> *He is on the path of life who heeds instruction, but he who forsakes reproof goes astray.*
>
> *- Proverbs 10:17*

## How Long Will This Take?

Everybody asks the question, "How long it will take to see results? How long before my rampaging toddler or preschooler regains the pleasant disposition he had as a baby and I can start enjoying him again?" Usually, it doesn't take long at all—a few hours to a few days to see a big change, then a few months to solidify this change—but with this proviso: **You must be consistent and diligent.** You must adhere fanatically to this checklist:

1. Watch your child closely, keeping him with you virtually one hundred percent of the time (Tomato Staking).

2. Correct him thoroughly *each and every time* he misbehaves, catching little things before they escalate into big things, outlasting him until your will wins over his.

Observe the above and you'll have a new family in a few months, even if you are starting late.

*Heed instruction and be wise, and do not neglect it.*
*- Proverbs 8:33*

## Turning Over a New Leaf

If you decide you want to try parenting the way I recommend in this book, please quit your present methods and undertake this with your whole heart. Don't confuse your child by picking and choosing between different and conflicting parenting styles or by changing methods completely every few weeks when you don't get instant perfection. Expect it to take a certain amount of time for both you and your child to learn new habits. Once you get the hang of it, and your child knows what to expect from you, he will respond very quickly.

The first few days will likely be the most challenging. Your child will surely put up some serious resistance, and since this approach will be new to you, your lack of confidence may encourage him to resist even more. Don't give up. Commit yourself to wholeheartedly applying Tomato Staking and teaching prompt obedience for at least three months. At the end of that time, sit down and take stock. Are things noticeably better? Has the need for discipline been greatly reduced? Are you enjoying your child more? If your child is still in the toddler or preschool age range, you should have almost no need for serious discipline by the end of the third month. Older children may have a few lingering problems that will need continued vigilance for some time, but by the end of three months you should find yourself mostly just giving instructions, teaching, reminding, and only very occasionally disciplining with more than a simple verbal rebuke. If good things are happening, let them encourage you to go on.

For school-aged children who have well-established bad habits and no real respect for their parents, it will take longer to reach their hearts and turn them around, but be assured that it *can and will* happen as long as you persevere. Your efforts will be rewarded if you remain steadfast in doing what is best for your child in God's eyes. Just do what you would do with a younger child: Keep them with you, then see that they do exactly what you tell them to do, without delay and with a good attitude. Instruct and correct as needed. Love always.

> *Pay close attention to yourself and to your teaching; persevere in these things; for as you do this you will insure salvation both for yourself and for those who hear you.*
>
> *- I Timothy 4:16*

## How We Began

We already had three young children, ages two, four and six, when we decided to follow the advice of some godly parents we knew and seriously undertake to train our children according to the good old-fashioned "Say What You Mean and Mean What You Say" philosophy. I did most of the training while my husband was at work. I started with all of our children simultaneously, but focused mostly on our two-year-old in the beginning, whose first "outlasting" session I described in the previous chapter.

I began watching him much more closely than I had ever watched him in the past. Each time I told him to do something, I worked to make sure he did it promptly, and without a bad attitude. I disciplined him as needed toward this purpose.

It wasn't easy for me. I had to be determined to be *extremely* consistent rather than *sort of* consistent. I had to be committed to making an *issue* out of everything he resisted me in, large or small. I had to make sure that when each conflict was over, I'd won, and that I'd won decidedly. But my efforts paid off. I only had one or two really tough sessions with him in the first few weeks and after that he seemed to miraculously accept my position of authority over him, and turned back into the cheerful, cooperative child he'd been at age one. Perhaps it was a relief to him to have someone else he trusted be responsible for guiding him through life once again, rather than having to assume the pressure of running his whole life himself.

As I was retraining the two-year-old, the older two children were watching. When they saw that I was serious about their little brother, they were considerably more reluctant to test me themselves. When they did test, they gave in sooner than they might have without having already seen my determined wins over their sibling. The hardest part was retraining myself to watch and consistently correct every time a correction was needed. But although that took determination and work, it was far easier than the constant power struggles that had characterized our relationship previously.

*Now therefore, my sons, listen to me, and pay attention to the words of my mouth.*

*- Proverbs 7:24*

## Training Opportunities

In the last chapter, I gave a few examples of things your baby or one-year-old should be able to learn. Here is a general list of things that any *toddler* can and should be expected to do, if he's been taught to obey. This list is not to be seen as a list of "tasks" to train for, but rather as opportunities to teach obedience. If you cannot depend on your child to do these and similar things regularly, with a cooperative spirit, then use these occasions to turn him around, and teach obedience and respect for you. In short, your toddler should obediently do anything you request as long as he is capable of doing it. That's obedience and that's really the only thing you have to teach him at this age.

Your toddler should:

- Understand that tantrums are absolutely forbidden.
- Come without hesitation when you call him.
- Stay near you when you tell him to.

- Hold your hand upon request, without pulling or letting go.
- Say or indicate, "Yes, mom", when you ask him to do something.
- Perform your requests without whining, crying, or pouting.
- Not misbehave in the car or in public.
- Remain quiet when you tell him to, or when you hold a finger up to your lips.
- Sit quietly next to you for as long as you want him to, without being bribed or entertained.
- Remain seated at the table until given permission to leave.

Don't expect your child to remember a long list of rules. Just expect him to obey promptly whenever you give him a simple direction. Don't hesitate to raise your standards and expectations. If your child disrupts church, acts like a terror in the store, can't be taken to a restaurant, or drives you crazy all day at home, your expectations of him are probably far too low. Believe in your child's abilities and possibilities and start training accordingly.

*A wise son makes a father glad, but a foolish man despises his mother.*

*- Proverbs 15:20*

## "All you have to remember is..."

I am not going to give a list of training opportunities for the next age bracket—older preschoolers up through the grade school ages. I think it is obvious to most parents by that time exactly where each individual child needs work. When in doubt, narrow it down to this: Your child can and should be expected to do anything you ask him to do, as long as he is capable of doing it.

Recently our family journeyed to Colorado and somehow I got arm-twisted into white water rafting with the whole gang.

Truthfully, I'd been dreading this event for weeks and was relieved to know that my adult niece was also having apprehensions. So there we were, standing on the riverbank waiting to climb into our assigned death traps, er, I mean, rafts. As we fretted over the cold and wet and the chances that our children might be tossed out of the raft and drowned, my nineteen-year-old son sidled up to us and set us both at ease. He winked, gave me a reassuring pat on the back, and said, "Mom, all you have to remember is the last thing the guide said to us: **'Pay attention to me and do what I tell you.'"**

There it is in a nutshell—exactly what I've been telling thousands of parents. You need not focus on complex rules or theories, or on training young children to perform a mountain of different tasks. Just train them to obey you. Train them to pay attention to you and do what you say. That's all there is to it! Just like the white water rafting guide said!

> *Be careful to listen to all these words which I command you, in order that it may be well with you and your sons after you forever, for you will be doing what is good and right in the sight of the LORD your God.*
>
> *- Deuteronomy 12:28*

## Aim at the Heart

Although I keep directing you to work on obedience, the real goal is a godly heart. You can never forget the heart, whether with a younger child or an older one. It must be the one thing you are always keeping your eye on. Obedience is just an easy straightforward key to reaching the heart and to changing it.

Now in order to reach the heart, we must teach ourselves to *see* the hearts of our children. Because the outside reflects the inside, we can often detect what is going on inside by watching the outside. Young children are usually open and honest with their feelings and cannot be cheerful on the outside unless they are truly happy inside. Older children may make more of an effort to disguise what's going on inside, but an observant parent will be able to see it anyway. So let the outward signs of a wrong attitude be your signal that your child requires correction. If you see anything other than *prompt, pleasant* obedience to a request, stop and fix it. In doing so, you will be taking great strides toward producing a godly child inside, not just creating the appearance of godliness on the outside.

> *And you shall love the LORD your God with all your heart*
> *and with all your soul and with all your might.*
> - *Deuteronomy 6:5*

## Mommy Radar

I have what I call "Mommy Radar." It goes off whenever I sense something needing correction. I'm not sure how I acquired Mommy Radar, but I suspect I've had it all along and just didn't know. What I thought was irritability was perhaps at times really the beginnings of Mommy Radar or Mommy Radar being ignored.

You see, it used to annoy me when my children whined, complained, or argued with me. It frustrated me when I had to request something multiple times before they'd do it, and it upset me even more when they would do it grudgingly. Slow obedience bothered me too, and sneakiness, and laziness, and so on. Because I was new in my parenting career, I thought that all these things that annoyed me were "normal" for children to do. I thought I needed to learn to somehow tolerate all of these until they "grew out of it."

Since then I've wised up. Now I know they won't *grow* out of it if I don't put some effort into *training* it out of them. If I want better behavior I'd better do something to make it happen. So now, if I find some behavior or attitude in my child annoying (my Mommy Radar going off), I recognize it as a sign that my child needs training. I welcome my Mommy Radar signals. They tell me to stop what I'm doing and promptly correct my child before these little behaviors escalate into bigger, more serious ones they will never "grow out of."

Instead of focusing exclusively on the big stuff, learn to develop Mommy Radar, becoming alert to all the subtle signs of a wrong spirit within your child. Watch the countenance of your children and notice when they won't look you in the eye, or when they smirk or pout. Notice that little stomp of the foot or their defiant body language when they pull away from you. Notice and act upon it when your Mommy Radar first alerts you. A stern word of caution, such as, "Take that look off your face," or "Don't roll your eyes at me like that," will avert later, more severe problems. If a firmer correction is needed, be prepared and give it. Nothing should be allowed to evade your radar because what it is picking up is your child's heart, *reflected* on the outside. If you Tomato Stake your child at this point, and correct him, you will be addressing his heart. And that's your chief goal.

> *The LORD looks from heaven; He sees all the sons of men; From His dwelling place He looks out on all the inhabitants of the earth.*
>
> *- Psalms 33:13-14*

## Our Oldest Child

Our six-year-old was typical of a "starting late" child. In the past he had always been fairly compliant, but I often had to "talk him into" obeying. He whined all the time and was very sluggish and lazy about how and when he'd get around to obeying. Yet he never threw fits or defied me directly, so I wasn't quite sure how to get tough with him. Should I spank him or not, for these many seemingly minor offenses?

I finally decided I had to do something before I woke up one morning and he was six feet tall and still grumbling and whining and feeling sorry for himself. I decided to make him respond correctly, cheerfully, and quickly every time I asked him to do something. Since everything else I'd tried had failed, I decided that when he didn't respond the way he should, I would have to spank, even if the issue seemed minor.

It was tough. He gave me about a dozen occasions to spank him the first morning of the "Big Change." Finally, about noon, he yelled at me that he "was going to go live with Aunt Faith!" I felt devastated. I felt heartbroken. I was shaken with uncertainty and doubt. Was I doing the right thing? Was I expecting too much? Was my child going to hate me forever? Should I go back to the low standards and failing methods I had been using before?

Well, I just couldn't quit. I had to listen to what my spirit was telling me and not relent. I had to persevere, at least this once. So I spanked him again and informed him that he'd better stick with me because his aunt "would not have put up with half" of what I had been putting up with! I admit that I raised my voice, which is not ideal. But I also gave him the firm impression that I was not backing down, that he was going to obey me and treat me with respect me, *or else*.

After things settled down a bit, I called our Christian mentors and with a shaking voice asked if I'd done the right thing. They said, "Well, if you got him that upset, you must have made an impression on him. Keep it up."

Apparently I did make a deep and good impression. He improved dramatically after that morning. Not only did he start obeying quickly and without whining, but he also became a happier child overall. From that noontime confrontation henceforth, I hardly ever had to spank him again. Now that he is an adult, he always laughs when I tell that story. He says that although he doesn't remember the incident at all, it must be the only time he ever really lost his temper. How wonderful to have an adult son who hasn't lost his temper since he was six years old! I have no regrets!

*Apply your heart to discipline, and your ears to words of knowledge.*

*- Proverbs 23:12*

# Our Second Oldest

Our second oldest was completely different from the other two children I've already described. She had been an independent, hyperactive, rambunctious handful ever since she began walking at the early age of nine months. I used to pray that she would "turn three" so I could be finished with the "terrible twos." But the threes arrived and they were as frustrating for me as the twos! Finally, she was four and a little improved, but not a lot. Clever and calculating, she knew how to get away with things. In particular, she knew how to discreetly deceive Mom and Dad.

At first, when she saw us disciplining her two siblings, she became outwardly meek and obedient herself. She was smart enough not to try the same things that were getting them all in trouble. But then we observed a few troubling things about her apparent obedience.

One night I took her up to her room to prepare for bed. I wanted her help in tidying up her room first, so I handed her a book and told her to put it away on the bookshelf downstairs. She scurried off and came right back. Then I asked her to put her shoes in the mudroom closet; again she quickly ran off to do what I said. So when she came back, I tucked her into bed and kissed her good night with a little hug and a "job well done."

Returning downstairs, I noticed the book, not on the shelf, but on the fireplace hearth *next to* the shelf. I thought perhaps she just misunderstood or forgot exactly what I'd told her. Then I noticed the shoes, setting neatly *outside* the closet door, not inside. That's when it struck me that she had not been obeying me with her whole heart. She had tried to get away with something—to only partially comply with my requests. She had intentionally misplaced those items in a way that she thought would not get her into trouble. Well, "almost" obeying is not obeying at all. I hated to do it, but I woke her up, spanked her, told her flatly that she had disobeyed, and I made her "fix" each one of her little "mistakes."

She was remorseful and I assumed she'd gotten the message until a few weeks later when she tried a similar ploy on Dad. Dad had decided that when he called, his children should come just as he had been trained to come as a child. They were to say, "Coming," and come immediately.

Since they were young, he decided to have them practice a few times first, before instituting this new policy. He gathered them together in the kitchen and carefully explained what he wanted. Then he sent them all to the living room to await his call. Upon hearing Dad's summons, the oldest obeyed perfectly. The youngest was next and also responded perfectly. But when it was her turn, our second oldest child said, "Come" instead of "Coming." Dad explained again that he wanted to hear, "Coming" and had them all try again. They all got it exactly right except, again, our four-year-old daughter. This time she said, "I come." Dad explained it again. The next time she said, "I'm coming." She couldn't seem to get it right.

Finally, both Dad and I caught on to her game. She was only being rebellious and sneaky. She knew exactly what we wanted, was very capable of doing it, yet was determined not to. Too smart to risk outright defiance, she had devised a more subtle form of disobedience.

So Dad got out the paddle. He did not get angry. He simply determined to correct the problem. He spanked her (one firm swat on the posterior, over her clothes), and then told her to try again. It took her six more tries (and six swats with the paddle) before she finally decided to obey and say, "Coming." Dad made her practice a couple more times just for good measure. And guess what? She *NEVER* defied us like that again! In fact she is extremely honest to this day, and cannot be outdone in zealousness to do the right thing. From that day forth, although still lively and enthusiastic, she became an absolute pleasure to live with.

*A man who loves wisdom makes his father glad...*
*- Proverbs 29:3*

## What to Avoid

As you work to turn your toddlers and older children around, be prepared for difficulties to arise. The following is an enumeration of some "Don'ts" of effective childrearing. Avoiding these will be essential to your success.

1. **Don't "distract" your child when you should be confronting him and disciplining him.** It's all right to distract a little baby at times, rather than train, but it is never okay to distract a toddler. When a toddler resists obeying you, "make an issue of it" until he submits, nicely and completely. If you distract him or move the forbidden object out of reach, you have taught him nothing—certainly not self-control. Once your child has complied, you can "redirect" his attention elsewhere as needed, but always make sure he has submitted to you completely first. Follow this one rule and you'll be ninety-nine percent of the way there with a little one.

2. **Don't do the modern "Time Outs," that are conceived as cooling-off periods that will miraculously return children to saintliness—without discipline.** They are misguided and unproductive. The heart is never altered by simply removing a child from temptation and placing him in a playpen or on a chair for one minute per year of age. If a child needs to "cool down," it is far better to stand him a corner facing the wall where he will be a bit uncomfortable. Keep him there for as long as it takes to motivate him to calm down and control himself.

3. **Don't ever send your child to his room as a punishment.** Leaving him alone allows him to stew over his plight, feel sorry for

himself, and grow bitter over this perceived injustice, or find other ways to ingeniously defy Mom. Instead, sit him right next to you where you can Tomato Stake tightly and effectively.

4. **Don't remove privileges as a punishment to correct or motivate a child.** Young children rarely relate well to anything but immediate correction. Delayed corrections and after-the-fact punishments just leave them feeling bitter or apathetic. After all, they've already lost their privileges anyway, so why repent? Rather than removing a specific privilege, come up with a closely related logical consequence, if you feel it will be effective and motivating. For example I might say, "Just now, you disobeyed me and rode your bike into the street. That is extremely dangerous. Because you did not obey me, you must come inside now." That is very different and works a lot better than saying, "No biking for the next two weeks," then allowing him to bike again two weeks later, whether he is repentant or not.

5. **Don't issue warnings.** Do not count to ten or to three or ever to two. If my child does not respond to my initial verbal instruction, I spank. It is quick, simple, and easily understood. No psychological mind games, no manipulation, no guilt. And for Mom, there's no anger, frustration, or fatigue.

6. **Don't "reason" with a child to persuade him to obey.** If I want to discuss my child's misbehavior, I do it after he has obeyed, not *in order to make* him obey. Too much explaining only encourages whining, arguing, and back-talking, leading to further rebellion and pride. Explain things, age appropriately, only after your child has shown a prompt willingness to obey *without* an explanation. A friend's husband recently observed that, "This is the way God teaches. He often doesn't explain until we obey. Then, He may or may not explain why He required what He asked us to do." Good point!

7. **Don't give children alternative choices to avoid a conflict.** It is better to welcome a conflict and teach obedience, than to defer it

until another day—a day that will surely come. The longer you wait, the more your child senses his power over you, and the harder the battle will be when you have to face it. Give choices only when your child is dutifully obedient on a continual basis.

8. **Don't become too dependent upon a "schedule."** Parents who are highly organized are often surprised when their usually well-behaved child suddenly loses control when forced from his accustomed routine. Why does this happen? Often it's because the child hasn't been taught to obey, but rather to conform to a strict schedule instead. He's grown accustomed to a rigid pattern of living and has even come to expect it as his "right." So when he misses his nap or his favorite afternoon snack, he throws a fit, demanding his "right" back, instead of respecting and obeying his mom. Order is a godly virtue, but be sure you are teaching flexibility as well. Vary your routine occasionally to achieve reliance on *you*, not a schedule. Obedience must always come first!

9. **Don't employ mind games to shame or manipulate a child into obeying.** Such manipulation will only prepare your child to eventually become a manipulative, insecure, passive-aggressive, angry, or self-centered adult. Many popular psychology-based techniques being used today are incredibly damaging to children by encouraging wrong thought patterns and habits. If it's wrong to manipulate other adults, don't teach a child to manipulate. Be open, direct, and straightforward, so your child will see your example and learn to do the same.

10. **Don't be a drill sergeant and a control freak.** Once your children have learned respect and obedience, give them lots of supervised freedom within the guidelines of godly behavioral standards. Be extraordinarily generous with your time, love, and affection. Be an extravagantly happy family. Discuss everything you do and think with your children. Teach them the ways of God by relating everything in life to Him and living accordingly. Once you are all getting along, roles are understood, and all the jostling for

power has ended, you can devote your time to teaching, nurturing, mentoring, and enjoying your children.

11. **Don't parent by the "Putting Out Fires" method.** This approach advises parents to overlook all the little misbehaviors and only correct significant infractions. That is many parents' picture of traditional Christian parenting and it is incorrect and ineffective. Tomato Stake instead.

> *Beware of the false prophets, who come to you in sheep's clothing, but inwardly are ravenous wolves. You will know them by their fruits.*
>
> *- Matthew 7:15-16*

## Outlasting

**Wynne:** What do you do when your toddler won't give in? I know he understands because he either grins or yells at me in his baby talk, then immediately tries to repeat the proscribed activity. Repeated training swats are ineffective, so I eventually relocate or distract him. After a week of this we have seen no improvement. Does he simply need more time?

**Elizabeth:** Each time you confront your child, you *must* win. If you don't—if you distract or relocate, or give in, or anything else—you've wasted your time. Your little one, in this case, doesn't need more time. Since he already understands what you want, it's clear he is just *refusing* to comply, knowing you will eventually cave in and not require obedience from him. Quit being a pushover. Outlast him. Every time he challenges you, let him know exactly what you expect and make sure that his little world stops until he obeys. Do not allow him to go *anywhere* or do *anything*, until he submits. An occasional swat during this will speed things up, but the key is to simply outlast him until he gives in.

The first outlasting session can take an hour or longer as I described with my third-born in a previous chapter. Do not quit.

Do not yield. Don't physically force your child to comply with your request. Don't yell or frighten him into obeying. Don't threaten. Don't get angry. Take your time. Maintain a firm "I've got all day and I will never give up" attitude. Keep pausing and then repeating your command. Space out occasional swats and give just one at a time, so you are not spanking too much. You must eventually outlast him to the point where he makes the conscious choice to obey you.

Once he has obeyed you, give him a moment or two to regroup, then test him to see whether he has submitted to you completely, or whether he merely consented to obey this once to escape his uncomfortable situation. Ask him to do some simple task, ideally something that would normally provoke his resistance. For example, you might follow up with, "Good, I'm glad you obeyed me. Now go pick up that book over there and put it on the table." Watch his response. Repeat with several other small instructions. If he refuses or resists any instruction, outlast him just as before. Don't quit until you are satisfied that he has submitted completely in his heart, and recognizes that you are his parent and he must ALWAYS obey you.

> *Cease listening, my son, to discipline, and you will stray from the words of knowledge.*
>
> *- Proverbs 19:27*

## Worse Before It Gets Better

As you are turning your child around, be prepared for things to get worse before they get better. Not every child will completely submit his heart and spirit to you after just one or two showdowns. Some children will continue to test you on and off for some time, hoping that you will eventually give up and go back to inconsistent "hit or miss" parenting. You must steadfastly persevere with Tomato Staking and all that is associated with it, until your child's heart has turned securely to you. When your child believes that you will never give in and allow him to control you again, that's when he will begin to truly yield his will to yours. That's when he will relinquish his independent and rebellious spirit, and will come to rest, with relief and peace, in the safety and protection of your love, guidance, and authority.

If intermittent disobedience is dragging on and on, it's because you have not yet fully convinced your child that you are his rightful God-given authority. He does not respect you and is just exerting his own power over you. The longer you put off convincing him, the worse it will get, so welcome his tests, knowing that each time you outlast and win, it will bring him one step closer to you and to God.

> *Judgments are prepared for scoffers, and blows for the back of fools.*
>
> *- Proverbs 19:29*

## "It's Not Working!"

If you've been Tomato Staking and training for obedience for a little while, and don't feel your efforts are resulting in much success, here is a short checklist of essential considerations to help you assess and remedy matters:

**Age of the child.** The younger the child, the more times he is going to "try it again." He is learning and wants to know whether you mean "stop doing that for now" or "don't ever do that again." A few repeats are necessary to explain things to him.

**Previous training methodologies.** The newer this effort is, the more times your child is going to test you. He wants to know which parenting method of the day is in force, so he can decide if disobedience is worth the risk. Persist in the methods taught in this book and the problem will resolve itself as your child eventually sees that you are sticking to one firm, just plan.

**Parental consistency.** The less consistent you are, the more times your child is going to challenge you. He wants to know whether you still remember the request made fifteen minutes ago. Are you really paying attention to him, and will you unfailingly discipline him for every infraction? Rigorous consistency will end any hope that a few petty violations will slip by unnoticed. Older children will be watching for consistency as well. If you are not consistent with them, they will deem it hypocrisy and unfairness and you will be unable to garner their respect by any means.

**Following through to success.** Failure to correct all the way to completion will only invite subsequent testing. You must persist until your child's attitude changes. The more diligent you are, the sooner the testing will end. When your child learns that disobedience—however trivial—is futile, the testing will stop. Allow even a tiny ray of hope that disobedience can triumph, and the testing will continue.

> *I do not write these things to shame you, but to admonish you as my beloved children.*
>
> *- I Corinthians 4:14*

# SIX

# DISCERNING THE SPIRIT

*Then the LORD said to Cain, "Why are you angry? And why has your countenance fallen? If you do well, will not your countenance be lifted up? And if you do not do well, sin is crouching at the door; and its desire is for you, but you must master it."*

*- Genesis 4:6,7*

## Once Order Is Established

Whether you started early or late, once you make it to the point where your children respectfully recognize you as their authority, you still can't quit. You still cannot place them on "autopilot" and let them go off unattended, expecting never to have to correct them again. Children will *always* need correction, teaching, and training. That's why God gave them parents—to head up the maintenance, advanced training, and educational programs.

As your child grows and changes, you will still need to be nearby to do this task God ordained for you. Never go back to allowing your child to routinely play for hours unsupervised. Don't expect him to raise himself; God gave you that job. After your child is under control and demonstrating consistent respect for your authority, Tomato Staking in its most intense form should no longer be needed.

But never abandon Tomato Staking completely. Let it evolve into a way of life where your children are always nearby with you mentoring them, rather than constantly correcting them.

Eventually, you will notice a new joy and freedom. With order established, you will stop feeling the frantic need to get away from your child for a little peace, and instead can begin to enjoy being with your child. You will find yourself wanting to undertake many things with them simply because you enjoy their company and enjoy teaching them the ways of the Lord. With the power struggles and major disciplinary issues out of the way, you can start the pleasant task of getting to know your child's heart better and begin guiding and shaping it toward the Lord and toward godliness. And you'll have the time to do it.

> *The father of the righteous will greatly rejoice, and he who begets a wise son will be glad in him.*
>
> *- Proverbs 23:24*

## Knowing God Helps Us Know Our Children

In order to woo your child's heart toward godliness, you must know God and His ways yourself. You must recognize and understand fallen, prideful human nature and its rebellion against God, and you must accept God's remedy—the perfect, sacrificial work of Christ, wrought by His crucifixion and resurrection.

Once that is accomplished, further knowledge and understanding of Scripture enables us to know the character of God, what He requires of us, what we are to emulate, and what we are to be teaching our children. Written to and about human beings, the Bible is saturated with examples of every species of behavior. It is our one essential divine textbook for understanding the hearts of both God and men.

This Biblical understanding of human nature enables us to reflect back on how we thought and acted as a child ourselves. If we can remember what we were like, it will help us to discern the deepest thoughts and motivations of our children. So make Scripture reading your constant habit. Let the Bible reveal to you God's heart; then let it reveal to you your own heart and then to help you in discerning and directing the hearts of your children.

*... the LORD weighs the hearts.*

*- Proverbs 21:2*

## Reading Little Minds

Is your child reflecting an accurate image of God? Is he thinking and acting as God would? Is he reflecting God's *character* in demeanor and action? If so, it's time for praise and nurturing. If not, it's time for correction and teaching.

My children's countenances constantly guide my parenting. If, for example I say, "Let's go now," and one of my littlest ones says "no," I don't jump on the word "no" and start disciplining. Yes, my Mommy Radar goes off, but I catch myself and immediately evaluate the situation. Usually, the child's tone of voice and facial expressions make things very clear. Sometimes body language is sufficient. What is his countenance telling me? What exactly did his "no" mean? Was his "no" simply an innocent expression of regret meaning: "But Mom, I'm having so much fun here I really don't want to stop now"? Or did it stubbornly mean: "I want to do what I want to do, and I'm not going to stop unless you *make* me stop"? I don't want to treat both of these responses the same, because the heart is different within.

In the first instance, the child's attitude is simply disappointment. There is no rebellion or anger involved. So I would simply instruct him pleasantly, "Don't say 'no' to Mama. You may tell me you are having a lot of fun and don't want to go yet, and you may ask, 'Can we stay a little longer?' But don't say 'No.' When I tell you to do something, I want you to say 'Yes, Mama.'" I might coach him further, teaching him by having him repeat it for me. There would be no need for discipline.

In the second case, where stubborn defiance is clearly evident, I would be much more firm in my response. I'd still say, "Don't say 'no' to me", but I'd also add, "Stop what you are doing right now, and do what I told you to." Then I would follow through, demanding prompt compliance.

As you Tomato Stake, constantly observe and discern your children's hearts, reading their thoughts and intentions. Compare them to God's character and if they are pure, nurture and teach. Encourage good attitudes with love and simple, kind words such as, "I like your beautiful smile today." However, if their hearts are less than pure, respond with appropriate training and instruction.

*The spirit of man is the lamp of the LORD, searching all the innermost parts of his being.*

*- Proverbs 20:27*

## Watch, Discern, Respond

Here's more on how this mind-reading works in everyday practice. Suppose I call my one-year-old to come. At the time I call, I may not really care if he comes or not. Perhaps I just want to offer a hug. If he doesn't hear me call, that's okay, since I may simply have wanted something easily deferred until later. Although I may not have an urgent need for him to obey, still, I naturally look to see if he heard, and I observe his response.

Suppose he hears me and stops, turns, and looks. What goes through my head? Suppose he pauses with no smile on his face. What do I think then? Suppose he turns and looks down at the toy he is playing with. What then? What do I think and do as I observe each of these outward signs?

Here is the same scenario again, this time with my thoughts included:

I call, "Jeffy, come here." Jeffy stops. I think, *"I know he hears me – will he obey me and come? What's he thinking?"* Jeffy looks at me with no smile. I think, *"He's not smiling. Bad sign. Perhaps he doesn't want to obey, or perhaps he still hasn't quite processed it all yet. I'll wait."* Jeffy turns back to look at his toy. I think, *"The toy is tempting him not to obey. He wants to keep playing with his toy. I'll give him another second or two to decide."* Jeffy begins pushing his car along the floor again. I think, *"I know he heard me and understands me. He's made his decision to ignore me and disobey. Time to correct him."*

Less than one minute has elapsed, but I have taken the time to accurately read my child's heart and let it guide my response. Even though it was not initially important whether he came or not, I now must correct him promptly. Why? I don't really care whether he comes, but I will always care if he is willful and disobedient or gives in to temptation. I will always care if he knowingly chooses to do wrong. Now I am not correcting him for not coming, I am correcting him for character issues. I am training him in godliness.

And so it goes with every correction I execute in my home. I make it a point to always try to accurately discern my children's motivations and spirit, and then to respond accordingly, with godliness in mind as my goal. Afterwards, I continue to observe and discern. If correction was needed, I watch their reactions. Did they understand my point? Do they agree with it? Are they resentful of my correction? Are they angry? Are they still proud and arrogant, but just faking a good attitude? My job is not complete until they have a genuinely good heart and a right spirit.

*Wisdom rests in the heart of one who has understanding, but in the bosom of fools it is made known.*

*- Proverbs 14:33*

## Let Attitude Guide You

**Vernita:** What do I do when my child stands there with arms folded and a pouty look, not directed at me, but at a brother who won't share a toy? His attitude is abominable. It's not just in sharing situations, but in other situations as well. Just now he was drawing with a pen on a big piece of paper. Making a mistake, he crumpled up the paper and in a VERY pouty way mumbled, "I can't make a picture." I sent him to the corner. This goes on all day, with him being pouty or grumpy over various trifles. I am Tomato Staking him and making sure I spend lots of time playing with him, hugging him, and loving him. So why is he like this and what do I do? Is it time for more drastic measures, such as spanking?

**Elizabeth:** Since he does this all day, it is very likely just a bad habit. At this point, I'd treat his depressed "looks" like any other misbehavior. Get his attention and say, "Straighten your face up." Educate him on the attitude and countenance he *should* have toward *anyone.* Then tell him what to do next: "Now smile, and share that toy nicely with your brother." Be sure he obeys.

From the "crumpled paper" incident you described, it is more difficult to ascertain his underlying heart attitude. Talk to him first to see his response and gauge it. Continue questioning and observing until you read his countenance and lay bare his motives, ascribing accurately a cause to his outward actions. This is truly crucial, since you cannot justly or successfully apply a correction when the underlying motive is unknown.

Knowing his motives will help determine how you should proceed. If he was just being cocky, I would correct with the issue of pride in mind. If he was just being habitually moody as usual, I would correct for that, telling him to change his attitude and making sure he obeyed. If he was complaining about having to work for something, I would correct, but focus my rebuke and correction on laziness (perhaps assigning more chores in the future, for example). If I thought that he really felt that he could never do anything right, I might not discipline at all, but rather have an encouraging talk with him. Motivation should always affect your response, so try to accurately discern motives before correcting.

*Correct me, O LORD, but with justice; not with Thine anger,*
*lest Thou bring me to nothing.*
*- Jeremiah 10:24*

## A Bad Attitude or Something Else?

Here's another example of mind-reading from my own household. One day my youngest child, four years old at the time, asked innocently, "When do I get to be the boss?" Hmm. Why would he ask that? What does he really mean? I said, "What?" a couple of times because I was stalling for time. I didn't know if this was a bad attitude that needed to be adjusted or not.

Finally my brain kicked into gear and I asked, "Why do you want to be the boss?" He said, "I dunno." I cheerfully helped him out with a few suggestions: "Because you like to give orders and boss people around?" He smiled and nodded, "Yes." I smiled and said, "That's not a good enough reason. You need a better reason before you can be the boss." He thought for a few seconds and then replied brightly with what was really on his mind, "If I was a boss, I could build a house." That caught me off guard and I had to quickly think some more. Perhaps he didn't just want to be bossy, but wanted to get something done. I said, "Yes, to build a house, you need a boss to organize the work to get the job done." This assessment satisfied him, and with that, he went merrily on his way, even though I hadn't actually answered his question!

Clearly, his motives weren't as bad as they first seemed to me. I'm glad that instead of scolding him, I took the time to discern his spirit correctly and learn that he just wanted to build something, not wield power over others. By probing his motives more deeply, I was able to teach good character without any need for discipline.

Don't just react to the obvious outward actions of your child, but also take time to notice the signs of the inner heart and spirit that are directing those actions. There may be a large reservoir of significant data below the surface that will make your nurturing and disciplining far more intelligent and to the point.

*Like apples of gold in settings of silver is a word spoken in right circumstances.*

*- Proverbs 25:11*

## Faking It

**Julia:** I am working on teaching my four-year-old to obey my first request, and have corrected her for obeying with a bad attitude. But sometimes I suspect she merely "pretends" to have a good attitude to avoid a negative consequence. Should I be concerned about this, or be satisfied that she "appears" to have a good attitude?

**Elizabeth:** What exactly do you require of her to demonstrate a good attitude? Are you focusing on some outward sign, such as an expansive smile, without being sure the inward heart has changed? To help you learn to discern her spirit accurately, study her face and body language carefully throughout the day for the clues to her inner thoughts. This may require time and patience, particularly if you are not used to watching for it. Watch her body language throughout the day, and try to correctly guess her next move. Try to recall what went on in your mind when you were a child and see if this helps you to follow her thought processes.

I am tempted to tell you not to ask her to do things that can be faked, like smiling. But the truth is, if you tell children to smile, and you watch their faces, you'll invariably see that as soon as they force themselves to smile, their attitude changes and the smile becomes genuine. Their entire countenance becomes bright, as it reflects their joyful hearts. This reaction is usually quite marked in a small child not yet experienced in lying or duplicity.

If you are certain her smile is "fake," then correct her. You might try saying seriously, "Smile a *real* smile now." That usually works. Little children are very intuitive and they know exactly what you mean. As soon as your child produces a genuine smile, reward her with your own genuine smile and a word of praise.

I would say, finally, that I do not require a cheery smile for everything. I want a good attitude, and a child can have a good attitude without producing a smile. Sometimes a good attitude is merely the absence of a bad one. If a child shows a willingness to obey, that is often enough to tell me that his heart is right and his attitude is good.

> *"Let your heart therefore be wholly devoted to the LORD our God, to walk in His statutes and to keep His commandments, as at this day."*
>
> *- I Kings 8:61*

## Don't Just Discipline—Teach

Godly parenting is not all about discipline and correction. That's just the part of the picture you need to get straight before you can go on to the more pleasant tasks of teaching and instilling values. Once you have your children under control, how do you go about teaching? You should be teaching by your own life example, of course, but that alone is not usually enough. You need to be talking with your children, and clearly communicating your thoughts and beliefs to them verbally. This should begin when they are little, with many one-on-one conversations between you. Later, you can expand this by letting them overhear conversations between you and your spouse or you and your older children. All that they hear will paint a picture for them of what you believe and will encourage them to believe likewise.

Perhaps we are a talkative family, but we have these types of conversations constantly at our house. We talk about what we've all been doing, where we've been going, and about all the human relationships that we stumble across in the course of our daily lives. We also talk about the world in general and make observation about all we see going on there. We relate all these things to the Word of God and how He teaches us in Scripture to live.

One perpetual theme in the conversations of our home is the character we see in ourselves and in others. We notice the attitudes and actions of others around us and discuss them when appropriate, as to whether they are good or bad. If good, we discuss how they please God and how we might emulate them; and if bad, we discuss the consequences. We often cite Bible stories offering examples of character qualities being displayed. Although the younger children are often just listening, we attempt whenever possible to include them in our discussions by asking them questions and explaining the main points at their age level.

We do not save up these conversations for only after our children have misbehaved. Nor do we allocate special times, such as during family devotions, to do this. Instead, we seize upon the endless opportunities that present themselves all throughout the day and use them to relate all of life to God and His divine plan for us. Make teaching your constant mindset and you will never want for endless opportunities to "train up your children in the way they should go." Be sure you do it with humility, not a prideful, gossiping spirit.

> *My son, give attention to my wisdom, incline your ear to my understanding; That you may observe discretion, and your lips may reserve knowledge.*
>
> *- Proverbs 5:1-2*

## The Fine Art of Lecturing

While most of our conversations are pleasant exchanges centered on how God's ways apply to each everyday situation, when our children do require verbal correcting, the tone of our conversation changes to a more formal lecture style to get our point across.

With small children, we keep our "lectures" very short—telling them what they did wrong and not to repeat it. As they grow, and as circumstances warrant, we do more questioning, instructing, and explaining—*always continuing until we feel there is understanding and agreement.*

**Marla:** How do you lecture children about an offense without making them feel overly guilty? Are there things you avoid? My husband grew up in a home where the children were controlled by making them feel guilty about everything. So, of course, he is highly sensitive to this, but ironically finds himself doing the same because he knows nothing else. I was raised in a "yelling" home, but we don't want that either. We are eager for your advice.

**Elizabeth:** The following four principles are key to effectual lecturing: 1. Discuss and lecture as needed, but never nag, whine, or attempt to manipulate with shame. 2. Carefully watch and read the heart of your listeners and KNOW WHEN TO QUIT. 3. After you sense genuine repentance, stop scolding and continue on in a gentle manner, with helpful instruction and love. 4. Do not end the session until peaceful harmony has been reestablished and your child has learned the lesson you wanted to teach.

If your child's eyes are glazing over with boredom, then you probably need to improve your lecturing skills. Ask thought-provoking, not guilt-laden, questions. Obtain some honest (but polite) feedback from them to be sure they understand and to be sure that *you* understand and are justly dealing with the situation. Ask them to search their souls and explain the motivation behind their conduct. Don't whine, pleading, "Whhhyyyy did you do such a horrible thing to me...." Instead, ask them, in a calm, matter-of-fact way: "Why did you do that? What was going through your head? Did you consider the consequences?..." Don't bulldoze over them, but wait for a thoughtful response to each question. Armed with the answer, you can now show them where their character and wisdom failed when they chose to do wrong. Patient questioning, coaching, and teaching—that's the proper way.

> *Search me, O God, and know my heart; try me and know my anxious thoughts; And see if there be any hurtful way in me, and lead me in the everlasting way.*
>
> *- Psalms 139:23-24*

## Lecturing Without Overkill

A while back, I had occasion to observe a well-meaning mom "lecturing" a child for a very minor infraction that the child had committed in carelessness. A quiet verbal reprimand would have sufficed, since the offense was not intentional, but the mom, in front of a group of other parents and children, decided to commit verbal assault instead. She angrily summoned the child, and accusingly asked a string of guilt-laden questions: "Why did you do that? Why didn't you see what you were doing? Why didn't you think the way any decent child would think? Why do you always have to be told what to do?" And on and on.

The child was mortified. He hadn't meant to offend. He was truly repentant. The parent was not satisfied with his tears and the repeated "I'm sorrys" he offered. The parent continued the torment by taking the child to another room where she could accuse, berate, and shame him all over again. Still not satisfied, the mom was starting up again for a third time, when I—unable to take this parental malpractice any longer—politely intervened, distracted the parent, and ended the torture.

As I reflected back on this episode, all I could think of was the word "OVERKILL." Please don't do this to your child. Quietly and firmly make your point and move on. When your words have touched your child's heart, STOP. Alter your demeanor to an appropriately pleasant or serious one, and continue with kindness and helpfulness, not condemnation. Both child and parent should be on the same side in the end, not one feeling guilty and shame beyond hope of redemption, and the other feeling triumphant, vindicated, and gratified. Whine, shame, or nag, and your child will soon begin to tune you out. Indulge routinely in overkill and be certain of this: your child will eventually become bitter against you. The risk is very real that the damage you wreak will be irreparable.

> *Only give heed to yourself and keep your soul diligently, lest you forget the things which your eyes have seen, and lest they depart from your heart all the days of your life; but make them known to your sons and your grandsons.*
>
> *- Deuteronomy 4:9*

## Discipline Without Overkill

Before I move on to a special chapter devoted entirely to Tomato Staking, I want to briefly warn against overkill in discipline itself. Many people assume that the word "discipline" always means "spanking." No, it does not. Neither does "correction" automatically mean spanking. There are many ways to discipline and correct, and you should only use what you need to use to achieve the effect you are seeking.

I never administer a spanking to a child who does not need a spanking. I never want any of my children to be terrified of me or my corrections. They won't be terrified if I treat them fairly, correcting only as needed and to the degree needed. If a simple verbal rebuke works, then that's all I use. If a lecture or a little time in the corner is needed, I do that. I only spank when I believe it to be the best way to deal with that particular child on that particular occasion. Again, everything depends on knowing my child and carefully assessing the situation as I proceed.

Here's an example of what I might do were I to catch a normally tender hearted, well-behaved child, in the act of disobedience:

**Mom:** *(Sees child going into the "off limits" cookie jar.)* "Go get the paddle."

**Child:** *(Appearing immediately sorry and worried, the child fetches the paddle because he's been trained to obey.)*

**Mom:** *(Sees that the child is agitated about getting a spanking. Mom knows that this is a more sensitive child than most, and that just being caught is punishment enough to motivate a change in future behavior, thus there's no need to spank. Instead, she switches to lecture mode.)* "What were you doing wrong?"

**Child:** "Getting a cookie."

**Mom:** "Didn't I say, 'No cookies until after lunch'?"

**Child:** "Yes Mom." *(Child has tears in his eyes and remorse written all over his face. He knows he has done wrong and is repentant.)*

**Mom:** *(Shows child the paddle.)* "Do I need to spank you to get you to remember what I told you?"

**Child:** "No, Mom."

**Mom:** "Stay out of the cookie jar. Do you understand?"

**Child:** "Yes, Mom."

**Mom:** *(Is satisfied that he is motivated not to transgress again, so she dismisses him with a direction.)* "Now go eat your sandwich."

Notice that no spanking was given. Whether or not you spank depends on whether or not you NEED to spank. Don't use spanking or harsh discipline automatically for everything. Once your children have made it through the initial training phase, you should not be spanking them constantly. Watch your child's heart and avoid overkill. Use discussion and lecturing to get your point across as needed. Remember that you want repentance, not resentment.

*"Oh that they had such a heart in them, that they would fear Me, and keep all My commandments always, that it may be well with them and with their sons forever!*

*- Deuteronomy 5:29*

# seven

# TOMATO STAKING

*Then I was beside Him, as a master workman;*
*and I was daily His delight, rejoicing always*
*before Him.*

*- Proverbs 8:30*

## So What Is Tomato Staking Again?

Every gardener knows what I mean by "tomato staking." A tomato plant grows fast, big, and wild. If left untended, it soon sprawls out into an unwieldy heap. As the fruit grows, it weighs the plant down to the ground. Propping by this time is too late. Any attempt to retrain and redirect the growth of the branches will result in breakage and substantial loss of the fruit due to rot, disease, and pests.

On the other hand, a properly cared for tomato plant will yield and produce an abundance of excellent fruit, with little or no loss. From the beginning it must be watered, cultivated, pruned, fertilized, examined for pests, and *staked up.* The branches will grow the way they were propped and trained, and when the fruit is large and ripe, the branches will have the strength to hold those beautiful tomatoes up off the wet ground. What a delight!

Think of your child as a tomato plant. Most parents provide too little staking for their growing young tomatoes. They care for them intimately when they are babies, but soon afterwards, begin letting them grow their own way. They feel uncomfortable assuming authority over their children and resort to the "Putting Out Fires" method of parenting. They try desperately to overlook misbehavior and avoid conflicts, unless forced into it by the magnitude of the offense or by their own anger.

Serious character flaws and bad behavioral habits, once established, are very hard to change, just like the neglected branches of a tomato plant. Catching problems now and then won't begin to make a dent in the problem. And just like the sprawling, unattended, unstaked tomato plant, there comes a point when it's simply too late. Your child's heart will become firmly fixed in the position it has been growing for all the many hours *in between* your sporadic corrections and over the years when you've allowed outside influences and peer pressure to do your staking job for you.

How much wiser to be your child's tomato stake from early on, keeping him close to you beyond infancy, training him constantly to be as you want him to be—a godly child and eventually a godly adult. If you prove to be a good tomato stake, when your child is grown he will be strong and secure in the godly ways you have trained him, and not easily persuaded toward the ungodly viewpoints and ways others.

Tomato Staking is a powerful tool enabling preemptive parenting. When you Tomato Stake, you can anticipate wrong attitudes and misbehaviors and prune them out of your child before they become ingrained habits. You can be right there to water and fertilize your child's heart by encouraging his efforts at good attitudes and right behavior whenever they are displayed. And, of course, it's easy to cultivate a close and loving relationship when you spend together the generous amount of time provided by Tomato Staking. Most importantly, a godly Tomato Staking lifestyle has the potential to yield in your child the fruit of faith and good character that he, in turn, will reproduce in his own children someday.

*...He watches all my paths.*

*- Job 33:11*

## Different Types of Tomato Staking

**Debra:** I'm confused. I have the idea that Tomato Staking is keeping children who show signs of being untrustworthy right next to you all the time, then gradually allowing them more freedom as they demonstrate they can be trusted. However, some people only keep a child with them for a short period of time when he has transgressed some specific command. They call this Tomato Staking too. Some practice the concept with all their children, whether trustworthy or not, while others, who also claim to be Tomato Staking, allow their children out of their sight for chores or play at certain times. So which of these examples conforms to your definition of Tomato Staking? Or do they all?

**Elizabeth:** While I do all of the things you described at various times, rather than thinking of Tomato Staking as a particular *technique*, overall, I practice it as a *lifestyle*. Usually my younger children are all within eyesight and earshot of me in the same room, even if they are behaving well. Right now, my five youngest, preschoolers to preteens, are just around the corner from me. I know exactly what they are doing and I can clearly hear them talking and interacting. Should they begin to bicker or get rowdy, I will stop them immediately. If they continue to misbehave, despite my verbal rebuke, I'll summon the offenders and sit them right next to me, allowing them to do nothing until they are bored stiff and motivated to obey. That would be more intensive Tomato Staking. Once under control and worthy of my trust again, I will direct them to some other activity closer to me than before, where I can see and hear them. That's still Tomato Staking.

My five oldest children, all teens and young adults, happen to be in another state at the moment. (Gasp!) If I did not trust them completely, they would be with me. I wouldn't say they are personally Tomato Staked any more at their ages, because they don't need to be. Even so, we usually aim at doing most things together as a family if possible, so what we do still conforms to the larger picture of a Tomato Staking lifestyle.

To further clarify what I mean by Tomato Staking, it may be helpful to divide Tomato Staking into several different types.

**Intense Tomato Staking:** Keeping your child within three feet of you (because he can't be trusted four feet or further from you), enabling you to "train" him to behave well, watching and correcting every infraction, and noticing and praising good behavior. After-the-fact discipline does not work nearly as well as the immediate discipline made possible by serious Tomato Staking such as this.

**Occasional Tomato Staking:** Keeping your child near you (how close and for how long depends on age and situation) to correct a repeated or habitual infraction. Here's an example: "Because you pushed your brother just now, and you know better, you must come inside and sit here quietly at the kitchen table while I cook dinner. You will not play outside anymore until I see a change in you and know I can trust you."

**Loose Tomato Staking:** This is for daily use with well-trained children. Younger children are always within eyesight and earshot, usually in the same room, but not necessarily right next to you. In this kind of staking, you do NOT send children to the bedroom to play where you can't see or hear them, relying on occasional checks to monitor behavior. When they are outside, you are with them, or able to see and hear them. You do not pack them off to the neighbors or elsewhere for an hour or two to play without your personal supervision. You do not sign them up for group activities that do not include your parental participation.

**Mentoring and Lifestyle Tomato Staking:** Elements of all the other modes are interjected briefly, when needed, into this type, and this type should always be used along with the others. Involving far more than training for behavior, and more than "discipline," this is a way of living that also involves mentoring, nurturing, loving, teaching, fellowshipping with, and abiding with your child. Here, you are not only keeping your child with you, but you are including your child in your day's activities.

You are building an intimate relationship with your child, teaching him to be like you in mind, spirit, beliefs and actions. You are diligently teaching godliness on the most basic, practical level. This is a lifestyle. This is our aim in our family and what I highly recommend to everyone else. If you employ the other types of Tomato Staking, but neglect this one, you will experience only partial success with your children. They may grow up being outwardly obedient, and perhaps even godly in their own hearts, but your children may not be fully equipped to reproduce godliness in their own offspring.

*Listen to counsel and accept discipline, that you may be wise the rest of your days.*

*- Proverbs 19:20*

## What Do I Do With Them All Day?

Many well-intentioned parents rise up in the morning, feed and clothe their young children, then send them off to play while they try to get all their household chores done single-handedly. Before long they become aware of arguing, bickering, shoving and pushing emanating from the play site. Crying and tattling follow close behind. Frustrated with the interruption, the parents scold and discipline, then send them off again hoping they will be able to finish their chores this time, but the cycle just begins all over.

Eventually, some of these parents decide to try Tomato Staking—living *with* their children rather than coexisting separately.

When they do, some of their first questions are: "What do I do with my children all day?" and "How will I get my housework done?" They've accepted the fact that their children need to be close to them, but they don't have the time to play with them all day and don't know any alternate course.

Rather than follow my children around all day, amusing them or participating in their play, I include them—even the toddlers—as much as is possible, in whatever *I* am doing. After all, the ultimate purpose of Tomato Staking is to teach my children to live and think as *I* do, and eventually grow to be godly *adults*. I think that's a lot better accomplished by having them follow me around, than having me follow them around.

If Tomato Staking is something new, or if the children are small, I often supply a toy to keep them amused while I do things that at first may seem boring to them. Very soon however, they begin to enjoy following me about, being my little "assistants." This role appeals far more to any young child than a mere toy, and the toy goes by the wayside. Children want their parents' attention above toys, and this is a way to get it.

As they tag along after me, I keep my eyes open for any small thing they are able to help me with. A toddler can pick up socks and put them in the dryer as I'm loading it. He can hand me forks and spoons for the dishwasher. He can help me pick up toys and clutter. He can throw items in the trash for me. Little children love to feel important and useful by helping Mom do these small tasks they view as pertaining to adults. All the while we are working, I talk to them, fellowship with them, and teach them.

Here are some other suggestions for things to do with your children in various routine daily situations:

**Meal Prep Time:** Many moms, new to Tomato Staking, find meal preparation times to be among the most challenging. While it might be necessary to put a baby in a playpen or give him to an older, responsible sibling to watch, most toddlers and preschoolers love to watch Mom cook. Let them sit up at the counter or table where they are close to you and under your direct supervision. Then, look for little ways to involve them. They won't always be able to help, but it's amazing how long they will be content to sit and watch as long as they know that you will very likely let them participate eventually in some small way, like stirring a mix or licking a spoon. Ask your little observers questions during the slow periods and explain to them all that you are doing.

**Yard Work:** At one time, I had a large yard with tons of weeds to pull, and several toddlers to watch at the same time. I gave the younger ones each a small garden tool to pretend to dig with (I told them where), and a small pail, and also set them to work collecting the weeds I was pulling. Even the littlest ones were delighted to walk back and forth picking up weeds and throwing them in their pail for me. Of course, when it comes to yard work, there's always plenty for the older ones—raking, planting, weeding, and mulching. If you just do it with them, they will come to enjoy it and you'll be Tomato Staking at the same time. Take a walk when you're done, or have a picnic lunch on the lawn, and they will be begging you to let them work in the yard every day all summer!

**Sewing:** I sewed dresses for my girls for years when they were little, with a baby on my lap and a toddler or two playing with my button box on the floor next to me. Slightly older children helped by cutting out patterns for me, or they made images with my scraps, or they designed their own pretend outfits with paper and pencil. At age eleven, my oldest daughter could actually sew and iron. We could finish a dress in half the time by working as a team. As a side benefit, I found this style of teaching by helping to be far more effective and pleasant than formal lessons!

**With Dad:** Dad can and should, if possible, be involved too. At our house, Dad includes the children in his office work by giving them small jobs, often with the older ones teaching the younger. Before long, everyone above the toddler age can run the fax machine, use the copier, and work the computers and calculators. Our oldest, by age thirteen, was handling all the computer support work for our in-home office as well as our official, out-of-home, business office. The older children take turns accompanying Dad to business meetings whenever possible. What amounts to a complex business education is all done informally here, by simply including the children in Dad's work.

You may not have a family business, but every Dad can find imaginative ways to do similarly. Whether it is mowing the lawn, washing the car, fixing a door knob, handling the family finances, or cleaning the garage, there's always a way to include the young ones, if you look for it. Everything is a precious opportunity to teach and mentor.

Sure, it would be easier to do it all yourself and you could probably do it faster and better, but what will your children have learned? Nothing. Worse than learning nothing, while you are managing the perfect house, your children will be off learning how to bicker, quarrel, and please themselves, grow independent and disloyal, and so on and so forth. And in the long run, is it really easier and faster to do everything yourself? Wait until you've Tomato Staked for a few years and you will come to appreciate the small amount of extra time it took to include your children in the routine of your daily chores. Suddenly you'll find you have a houseful of responsible, trustworthy children who know how to manage and organize, who appreciate the value of hard work, who accept responsibility gladly, and who take pride in being a productive hardworking member of their family—and you can relax a little!

*The wise of heart will receive commands, but a babbling fool will be thrown down.*

*- Proverbs 10:8*

# Should I Start With One or All?

**Leigh:** We are a homeschooling family with several children who are not well trained, and I want to start Tomato Staking them. Should I pick one to concentrate on or stake them all at once?

**Elizabeth:** Sometimes I suggest Tomato Staking the worst-behaved child first, but ordinarily, it is best to start all of them at once. If you feel insecure about this, focus on the worst child for a few days, then collect all of them and continue from there.

Remember, this is a lifestyle, not a quick fix. You can't Tomato Stake one child for a few weeks, then drop him and move on to the next child for a few weeks. If you try this, the first child will regress immediately, because he'll know your new rules are temporary. You will then be worse off than before you started.

Since you are homeschooling, take advantage of it to help make Tomato Staking easier. Let your schooling provide structure and order for a portion of the day. Have the children you are teaching get their books and sit at the same table with you where you can supervise and tutor as needed. You can sit a baby on your lap or put him in a playpen or let him play on a blanket on the floor near you. With older preschoolers, I usually give them coloring books and crayons, or perhaps something like Play-Doh to amuse themselves with, requiring them to sit at the table with me also. This way I can keep them closely staked and learning to be respectful, considerate, orderly, quiet, and obedient. (This is wonderful preparation for behavior in church and other public situations, by the way.)

Expect all of them to remain quietly in their seats unless they have permission from you to do otherwise. Don't be afraid to interrupt your schooling at any point to correct violators. If fact, make this your TOP priority. So, if signaled for quiet, and they begin talking, stop your schooling and correct them. If a child gets out of his chair, stop immediately and correct him.

A persistent troublemaker can be required to quietly stand in a corner facing the wall until he is motivated to behave. The more vigilant you are in the beginning, the easier it will be thereafter. You need to send the unwavering message that obedience comes first, before homeschooling lessons or anything else. If obedience really does come first in your home, you'll find that homeschooling will soon become comfortable and enjoyable, no matter how many children you have.

*He rules by His might forever; His eyes keep watch on the nations; let not the rebellious exalt themselves. Selah.*
*- Psalms 66:7*

## Group Tomato Staking

Occasionally, when I've been too busy or undisciplined (shame on me) to properly attend to my children, some of the younger ones will become unruly and overly loud. When this happens, I call everybody over and park them on the couches and chairs in my family room. I instruct them to be silent and sit still. If they persist in teasing, wrestling, poking, tickling, and laughing, I separate them further, still keeping them all in front of me. They are not to touch each other and are corrected if they do.

If a couple of them persist in pestering each other, I make them sit back-to-back on the floor close to me, not touching or even looking at each other. If my words are ineffectual, and a child needs physical discipline, I do not take him to a different room, lest the others act up while I'm gone. If a spanking is needed, I do it right there. This little drama usually sobers the others into alertness and obedience. I separate, discipline, and outlast, until all are paying attention and cooperating.

It may take a little while for them to realize I am serious, but once order has been restored and maintained for a reasonable period of time (until I know they've decided to stop fooling around and are ready to start taking me seriously), I begin slowly releasing *one child at a time,* briefly, with an assignment. I give a specific task, then watch to see that it is obeyed. If there is any doubt about the child completing his task and *returning promptly,* I don't send him anywhere out of my sight.

Then, I just expand this further and further. At first I'm just sending one child at a time off to do a quick task and return. Later it's two at a time doing separate tasks, then more children, then longer tasks, and so on and so forth. It's important to note that in the end, I am not back where I started, with everyone going off in different directions doing as they please, and me running around frantically trying to keep track of everyone. Nope, this time I keep things more orderly and under control. I don't progress past any point where I begin to have problems. I revert back to requiring couch time for any child who cannot be completely trusted to obey. In the end, I have them each doing what *I* want them to be doing, in an orderly, respectful way.

Now this regrouping could take a half hour, several hours, or even all day, depending on what state of chaos things have deteriorated to and what training they have had previously. If you are applying this idea of group Tomato Staking to children who have had little training in the past, then expect this to take several hours or perhaps even several days initially, just to get to the point where you can begin giving out individual assignments. Expect to need to "regroup" repeatedly for at least three months. Remember, you must aim at a Tomato Staking lifestyle, not the previous "every man for himself" program.

> *"And it will come about that as I have watched over them to pluck up, to break down, to overthrow, to destroy, and to bring disaster, so I will watch over them to build and to plant," declares the LORD.*
>
> *- Jeremiah 31:28*

# Really Watching Your Child

**Anne:** I am trying to follow your instructions for Tomato Staking with my two-year-old, but I'm running into a problem. For the most part, she is sweet, happy, and obedient, but there are a few things that discipline doesn't seem to cure. Her favorite disobedience occurs when I have her on a chair beside me in the kitchen while I'm cooking. She knows she is supposed to stay away from the sink, but she invariably disobeys and turns the faucet on and splashes in the water. I correct her for this, yet the next minute she is doing it again! It doesn't seem to matter that I am right there with her and that I consistently spank her each time. Help!

**Elizabeth:** Although you may think you are Tomato Staking and being consistent, from what you are telling me, you are not. Let me explain. When you have her sitting at the counter with you, how is she able to turn the water on and start splashing without you seeing her? I can understand it happening once initially when you aren't expecting her to go for the faucet, but by the second time, you should have caught her before her hand ever reached the handle. That's what I mean when I tell people to watch *carefully* and catch and correct *immediately.*

Here's a picture of how this should look and what you should do. First, put her up on the chair near the faucet. Stand so that you can always see her while you are making dinner. Glance at her every few seconds like you would glance in your rearview mirror while driving. Give her some measuring cups or a toy to play with and tell her clearly not to touch the faucet. Then "lie in wait." You are ready and waiting to teach her something.

You see her leaning toward the sink out of the corner of your eye. You turn your head slightly so you can see her better without her noticing that you are watching. She begins to reach for the faucet. Since she is used to getting away with things, at least for a few minutes, she doesn't even notice that you are creeping up behind her. You give her a quick, surprise swat on the bottom just as her little hand reaches the handle. Startled, she sits back down quickly and looks up at you. You look her sternly in the eye and tell her, "Don't touch that faucet again."

She goes back to her toy, and you return to your cooking. This time, you are *really* watching her and getting ready for a repeat. Only cook if it doesn't get in the way of your parenting. Discipline yourself to have the mindset that training your child always comes first.

In a minute or so, she glances over to see if you are watching (you pretend you are not), and then she reaches for the faucet again. If close enough, ambush her with a swat immediately. If you are a few steps away, calmly walk over, pick her up, turn her over your knee, and give her several "I mean business" swats on the bottom. Then set her back firmly in her chair and repeat: "*Do not* touch that again. Do you understand me?" Then remain right there, ready to enforce your order. Move away only when you sense by her countenance that she is ready to submit to your authority.

REPEAT AS FREQUENTLY AS NEEDED to convince her that you are always watching her and that she must obey you. If she is resistant, stand her in a corner for a few minutes to think over her options before allowing her to sit at the counter and try again. Sometimes, simply stop what you are doing and look her right in the eye *before* she tries something, as if to say, "Make my day." If she asks for a showdown, give it to her and win. Do this with *everything* you tell her to do all day, as needed, and you *will* see a change, usually in short order.

> *Set a guard, O LORD, over my mouth; keep watch over the door of my lips.*
>
> *- Psalms 141:3*

## Tomato Staking vs. Consequences

**Cynthia:** Our son is ten and is always in trouble! We punish him for his actions with a specific pre-designated consequence each time, but he "forgets" rapidly or shrugs it off. At the rate he is going, he will be grounded his entire life! He's probably thinking, "*Why not just disobey? I'm grounded anyway!*" We pray, we talk, we train, we read, we seek outside wisdom, all to little effect. What do you do with a child who is unfazed by the threat of certain punishment for misbehavior?

**Elizabeth:** Forget about pre-designated consequences as a tool for training. You have just illustrated a primary reason why I rarely, if ever, discipline this way. First, the consequence is delayed, and therefore far less effective. Second, when you tell your child in advance, what consequence he will receive for what specific disobedience, all you are doing is allowing him to decide if the disobedience is worth the consequence. Maybe he will think it is. Disobedience should never be an option; he must obey, no matter what.

Tomato Stake this child! Keep him with you constantly and re-educate him. Reward cooperation with your approval and fellowship, but be pro-active in disallowing all misbehavior and bad attitudes. Correct him before he has the opportunity to commit offenses that are worthy of major discipline. If and when a consequence is needed, it should always be given *along with* requiring him to obey. Consequences should logically match the specific situation and should be varied according to the repentant or unrepentant spirit of the child at the time he is being disciplined.

While I don't recommend routinely removing privileges as a consequence, you should withhold virtually all privileges from a chronically misbehaving child. Tightly Tomato Stake him, then grant freedoms and privileges one at a time as he earns them with continued good behavior and positive attitudes. Most parents err in allowing too many rights and privileges before they are merited by the child's responsible, good behavior.

> *Obey your leaders, and submit to them for they keep watch over your souls, as those who will give an account. Let them do this with joy and not with grief, for this would be unprofitable for you.*
>
> - *Hebrews 13:17*

## The Challenging Child

Don't despair if you have a difficult child. You're not alone. I myself had one such child. He was happy, enthusiastic, and smart, but also hyperactive, lacking in self-control, impetuous, careless, and seemingly oblivious to whatever kind of discipline I used. It took him months to learn the same lessons my other children absorbed in days.

When he was two and wasn't responding like the others had, I was discouraged. Nothing seemed to work. I was correcting him promptly for every infraction, but it just wasn't enough. He'd do the same things over and over. Every temptation was an entirely new experience to him, seemingly unrelated to past corrections. He simply followed the urge of the moment.

I finally realized that a higher degree of Tomato Staking than was used on the other children was the answer. Still, after a few weeks, I saw little difference. Rather than capitulate, I determined to persist. I resolved to Tomato Stake him until he was twenty if that's what it took to prevent an out-of-control child from becoming an out-of-control adult.

So that's what I did. I kept him *tightly* staked to me from that day forward. If I drove to the store, he went with me. If I wanted to sew, he sat on the floor next to me and played. If I wanted to nap, he napped on the bed right next to me too (whether he was tired or not). If he wouldn't sleep at night, I sat next to him, insisting he lay still until sleep came.

I wasn't angry with him, or overly strict. In fact, I enjoyed him immensely most of the time. I just kept him constantly close to me so I could foresee problems and promptly correct him. I wanted him to know that obedience was not a one-time event—he had to *keep* obeying me. Even when he was displaying self-control, I kept him Tomato Staked so I could get to know him, enjoy him, and encourage him.

Yes, I spanked him. Over the next few years, he received more spankings than all the rest of my children put together. I never came close to breaking his bright spirit (and didn't want to), but he did eventually progress to the point where he'd become serious and get a little repentant tear in his eye when I'd scold him. Spankings were seldom needed after that. Eventually, he started thinking ahead—just a little, then a little more. By eight years old, he was generally trustworthy, enabling me to loosen the reins now and then, to see if what he'd learned was "sticking." Today, I am extremely glad I invested the considerable effort it required to train this child when he was small. I'm thrilled with the happy, obedient, enthusiastic, and trustworthy young teen he has become.

*I will instruct you and teach you in the way which you should go; I will counsel you with My eye upon you.*

*- Psalms 32:8*

## Just Keep Tomato Staking

**Mia:** I want some straightforward answers. I have been following your parenting recommendations, but my son Carl, now three, is still making my life a challenge, driving me and everyone else crazy. Here are some typical problems:

He can't stay on task and has zero attention span. I will tell him to look at me, and after a few seconds, he will avert his eyes. I will hold his chin, instruct him to do something, then ask him what he is to be doing, and he will have *no clue*! He moves and touches constantly. I really think his hands and feet aren't connected to his brain. If I tell him to not touch, two seconds later he is touching again. I'm reduced to tears in the store, trying to prevent him from touching everything.

Just as disturbing is that he cannot keep his hands off the baby. Recently, I took him with me to the hospital for an ultrasound on the baby. Well, he refused to stop leaning into the stroller to hug his brother. Every time my attention was diverted, he was right in the baby's face, assuring him, "I know you don't want to go to the doctor, but it'll be okay. Be a big boy." The baby was frightened and started to cry, prompting the big brother to hug him even tighter. I became uptight and nervous, as I struggled to comply with the hospital red tape while keeping the lid on him at the same time.

He usually obeys immediately and joyfully when I ask him to do something, but the problem is this: he doesn't KEEP obeying for longer than a minute. I'm concerned he just isn't remembering or thinking. How do I get him to learn this? I'm seeing no *lasting* results. Quite frankly, I am discouraged by the impossibility of achieving lasting results without constantly hovering over him to rein him in. I could correct him a hundred times and he would STILL persist in some forbidden misbehavior. HELP! What else can I do?

**Elizabeth:** Yep, sounds familiar. I'd love to give you a 'quick fix' answer, but I don't know any. I don't believe one exists. This has to do with the inborn personality of your child. Think of him as a diamond in the rough. God has given him some wonderful underlying qualities (enthusiasm, determination, steadfastness, persistence, etc.) that, if neglected, will lead to disaster, but if honed and polished, will become something truly beautiful. If you want to eventually see that he becomes the best he can be, you will have to dedicate yourself to making his training your full time job for as long as it takes.

Sometimes you won't see major improvement in this type of child until he is about six or so, and then only with constant Tomato Staking. Just keep on Tomato Staking as closely as you can. Focus on his impulsiveness, stopping him constantly BEFORE he does something, deliberately instilling the habit of stopping and thinking first, before rushing headlong over the next cliff. Talk to him and pleasantly, but seriously, question him: "What was it that you were about to do? Do you think that is a good idea? What do you think might happen if you do that? Do you think I will like it if you do that?" Each time he begins to get out of control, stop him and make him sit quietly next to you until he calms down. Then proceed with watchful direction and instruction.

Include him as much as possible in what you are doing. Teach him how to put all that energy and wonderful enthusiasm to good use. Watch his heart and encourage all the good you see. Use praise for those things as a springboard to motivate him to control his actions ("I know you love your brother, so be careful not to squeeze him too tight or you will hurt him.") Persevere!

*But what I am doing, I will continue to do….*
*- II Corinthians 11:12*

## Tomato Staking For Fun

**Carrie:** I love reading on your website about all the positive results parents have achieved with Tomato Staking and I want to achieve the optimum success with my thirteen-month-old son. I want to train him as opposed to waiting for something to "happen" first. I believe these are proper principles, but I also need advice on how to balance discipline and love. I'm afraid that I am too often focused on looking for misbehavior, on correcting, and on disciplining, and not often enough enjoying my child.

**Elizabeth:** When I tell people to "watch" for misbehavior, I want them to *notice* misbehavior and wrong attitudes rather than overlooking them. A parent should never over-analyze and attribute wrong to their child's every action. Along with noticing the wrong their child does, they should also be noticing the right and looking for ways to encourage that—a habit that should, indeed, be enjoyable.

As far as "balancing" discipline with loving your children, there's really no equal or preset "balance." You should *always* be enjoying your children *until* you see something requiring correction. When that happens, you stop, correct, then return to enjoying them.

Initially, if your child has not been trained to obey, and is being perpetually rebellious, you may be doing a lot of disciplining and little enjoying. But if you are diligent, this phase should quickly pass—a few hours for some children, a few days for others, and, for an older child or a stubborn one, a few weeks.

After that initial training/retraining period, you should be spending virtually *all* your time enjoying your child as you continue to supervise and monitor. In the midst of enjoying your child, you should be pausing only occasionally and briefly for correction and training. And, of course, you should always be loving, even in the midst of discipline.

> *A wise son makes a father glad, but a foolish son is a grief to his mother.*
>
> *- Proverbs 10:1*

## Growing Up Staked

**Elizabeth:** Louise, I've known your family for years and have seen the wonderful results of a Tomato Staking lifestyle focusing on character and the goal of godliness. How about sharing a few examples of how Tomato Staking was applied in your home as you were growing up?

**Louise:** My father and mother believed that children should learn about life from their parents, not from playmates or schoolteachers. So in our family, Tomato Staking was primarily a positive mentoring method used to mold and shape the character of the child. Occasionally, it was used as a tool for discipline, similar to being grounded, but was often a much longer-term arrangement, with the child being kept near the parents, not sent to his room.

In my house, the *thought* of being tightly Tomato Staked was actually more troubling to the child than the actual staking. After all, what's not fun about having the undivided attention of your mother or father? Basically, the Tomato Staked child hung around the parent all day. If my father were working on a car, the staked child would be there, handing him tools, asking him questions. Dad would explain what he was doing, and invite him to try himself. If our parents had to attend a meeting, the staked child would be brought along, sitting quietly while listening to the adults' conversation. Afterwards, the parent and child might discuss what was said as part of a conscious plan to teach and shape. This close interchange between parent and child fostered significant learning, including how to think and reason.

It's easy to feel sorry for a child who is being tightly Tomato Staked, because he is being denied some freedoms enjoyed by others. But in my house, the child who was Tomato Staked was really getting the most and the best of his parents' time and attention. He was really the "favored" child. What can be better than that?

> *I am the LORD, I have called you in righteousness, I will also hold you by the hand and watch over you, and I will appoint you as a covenant to the people, as a light to the nations, to open blind eyes, to bring out prisoners from the dungeon, and those who dwell in darkness from the prison.*
>
> \- *Isaiah 42:6-7*

# eight

# THE 'S' WORD

*Do not hold back discipline from the child, although you beat him with the rod, he will not die. You shall beat him with the rod, and deliver his soul from Sheol.*
*- Proverbs 23:13-14*

## Is Spanking "Hitting"?

Secular sources today typically condemn all spanking as barbaric. Occasionally, a solitary voice will allow it as a last resort. Most of the Christian parenting authorities either gloss over the subject, or else teach the disagreeable style I call "Ritual Spanking." Between scarce information and conflicting, often erroneous opinions, young Christian parents are understandably confused. Hence, although I would like to skip this chapter, I can't.

Beware of the popular definition of spanking as "hitting," deceptively implying child abuse when proper spanking is nothing of the sort. For thousands of years, wisely applied spanking has been considered a mandatory part of good parenting. But suddenly, in the last generation, permissive parenting gurus have sprung up everywhere, denouncing the practice as teaching violence to our children.

Millions of parents have fallen blindly under the spell of these alleged experts, accepting their assertions as fact, and ceasing to use this essential tool. Meanwhile, as fewer parents dare to be politically incorrect and spank, the rate of violent crime in our country has exploded—*especially* the rate of juvenile violence against parents. Could there be a connection? If anyone is in doubt about the effects of the modern "gentle" parenting style on the juvenile crime rate, I would strongly urge them to read the book No Fear, by Robert R. Surgenor. It is filled with statistics and solid evidence derived from the author's nearly twenty years as a detective in charge of juvenile crime for an Ohio police department. Perhaps it is the *lack* of spanking that teaches violence, not the opposite.

Any child can tell the difference between a just spanking and hitting. The simple, all-essential difference between hitting and spanking is this: Hitting is done in anger and its goal is injury and retribution. Spanking should never be done in anger, should never injure, and has the goal of training for the good of the child.

> *Those whom I love, I reprove and discipline; be zealous therefore, and repent.*
>
> *- Revelation 3:19*

## When All Else Fails

With their hearts and the Scriptures telling them to discipline, but society constantly making parents feel guilty about spanking, many have chosen the middle ground by purposing to use spanking "only as a last resort." This is serious error. When this practice is adhered to, we wind up with parents who hold off spanking until they are overcome by anger and frustration. Then they lash out in rage and vengeance. That's never the proper way to spank. Not only is it cruel and damaging, it is also ineffectual, as it shifts the issue from the child's misbehavior to the parent's lack of self-control.

Those spanking in anger must examine their parenting to see if they have allowed misbehavior in their children to go too long uncorrected. Never defer spanking until you've lost your temper. Watch your children and correct minor disobediences and bad attitudes early, with a spanking if necessary, and you won't experience the frustration caused by a child who provokes you to lose your patience and temper. Do not spank only as a last resort.

> *He who is slow to anger has great understanding, but he who is quick-tempered exalts folly.*
>
> *- Proverbs 14:29*

## Avoid the "Ritual Spanking"

The "Ritual Spanking" taught in some Christian parenting circles entails taking the offending child and a Bible to a separate room every time a spanking is needed. The child is given a talk, spanked a specific number of times or until he cries, then required to voice a formal apology. The ritual ends with a religious speech and a prayer.

Reject both the principle and method of this type of spanking. There is no need to exit to a separate room. Spanking young children in front of siblings causes little, if any, embarrassment. Small children are not easily embarrassed. If they *are* slightly embarrassed, it may deter the misbehavior that led to the spanking. Spanking in front of siblings will also encourage those siblings not to commit the same offense.

Spank without explanatory or apologetic lectures. *Do not* say, "Mommy loves you, and she really hates to spank you, but you made Mommy sad by doing that, and I know you didn't mean to do that, but...blah, blah, blah." Children know intuitively that if they can elicit the justifying lecture, they've won your sympathy and with it, power over you. They know that you are not really convinced that they should be punished at all, so the punishment won't be as severe as it ought to be. They will have little motivation to change their behavior.

Afterwards, don't shower the spanked child with hugs and kisses and more apologies: "Now honey, Mommy loves you anyway, even when you disappoint Mommy, and Mommy doesn't want to spank, but God says she must, but Mommy forgives you...." This vacillating approach shouts of the insecurity you feel in disciplining. Don't make it sound as if you personally hate to do it, but God is forcing you to be a mean mommy and spank. If you don't believe you should spank, then don't spank. If you believe that appropriate spanking is good and right, then do it without apology, and without blaming God or anyone else.

It is far wiser to emphasize that neither you nor God is pleased, and you meant business with that spanking, and that the antecedent misbehavior *will not* happen again. You may tell your child that you don't like to spank him, but be sure he knows that you most certainly will, if a his behavior warrants it.

To give small children a spiritual lecture or pray with them after spanking is a dubious practice. Lecturing and teaching are necessary and important, but be sure that you are not doing it inappropriately. When a simple swat on the rear is being used to training a young child, usually no long spiritual speech is needed. It will be incomprehensible overkill. In an older child, lecture in order to instill wisdom, not to humiliate or badger.

This is not to say that you should never quote Scripture to your children or discuss spiritual things in accordance with their age. Quite the opposite. Do so, but don't save it up for discipline time. Instead, fill all of your daily life with God's words, ways, and teachings. If the teaching of godly wisdom is done pleasantly and properly throughout the day, when your children are behaving well, a special lecture usually won't be needed when they occasionally disobey. A few words of rebuke should suffice. Serious lectures should be reserved for serious offenses or for children who are slow to repent.

*The commandment is a lamp and the teaching is light; and reproofs for discipline are the way of life.*

*- Proverbs 6:23*

## Three Types of Spanking

Now that I've criticized several modern approaches to spanking, I will detail three types of appropriate spanking, which I consider "wise reproof."

**The Training Swat.** This is a painless pat with the open hand to the diapered bottom of a child, helping to make the connection between "no" and what he is doing. It may also be used to ambush an otherwise trained child who is on the verge of giving in to a temptation. It generally means: "Pay attention; I'm talking to you," or "Stop! Now choose to do what is right." If the child does not respond, it can be applied more firmly. One swat at a time, with a pause between each, should do. Take your time, and combine with "outlasting" and repeated instructions.

**The Reminder Swat.** One firm swat to the clothed bottom of a deliberately disobeying toddler. Repeat after a pause, if the child continues to disobey. This swat can also be used to "ambush" a child who thinks you are not looking. A paddle may be used if the parent prefers, or if needed to make a bigger impression. You need not spank hard with a paddle. In fact, much less effort will achieve the same results.

**The "I Mean Business" Spanking.** This is typified by one to perhaps three stinging swats to the clothed bottom, delivered with a firm hand or a paddle. This spanking is reserved for repeated or serious misbehavior committed deliberately by an older child. The offending child is required to bend over and place his hands on a chair, safely out of the way. If the child resists, the parent should outlast until he complies. When the child is ready, one or two meaningful swats are given. A lecture and other measures (such as

Tomato Staking) should usually accompany this type of spanking. "I Mean Business" spankings are never for wee ones.

Let me add a few precautionary words. Never spank anywhere but on a covered bottom. The bare hand, used with prudence, suffices for the very little ones. If you are dealing with a rebellious toddler or older child, however, a mom's hand may be insufficient. I have used a flat wooden paddle upon occasion, and find it suffices. Interestingly, when I use a paddle, I am less inclined to spank hard, because a mild paddle swat is more effective than a forceful swat with the open hand. Because a swat with a paddle requires very little physical effort, I can remain more relaxed and calm while disciplining. Never, never spank in anger.

*A fool rejects his father's discipline, but he who regards reproof is prudent.*

*- Proverbs 15:5*

## The Child Who Resists

**Betty:** My six-year-old son refuses to receive his spankings obediently. He knows that if he does not humbly submit to one swat, he will receive another. Yet he *fights* me and will not turn around to receive his spanking. I don't want to misdirect the swat because of his twisting, nor do I want to have to pin him to the floor to get the job done. I wind up becoming angry about all of this, and that's wrong.

**Elizabeth:** When he needs a spanking, tell him so. If he protests, tell him to be quiet. If he continues, tell him he will now receive another swat for arguing. Then tell him to bend over, place his hands on a chair, and assume "the position."

If he still refuses, argues, or writhes about, calmly tell him that you will not wrestle with him, but that he will not be going anywhere or doing anything until he submits to the number of swats you decide that he needs. Warn him that the more he rebels, the more he will be asking for discipline. Then pull up a chair and wait. Restrain him only if needed to prevent him from running off. Outlast him as you would for any other misbehavior. Some "corner time" may speed up the process.

Eventually he will weary of crying, whining, and falling on the floor. When you sense this approaching surrender, ask him if he is ready to obey. If he assents, tell him to place his hands on the chair and bend over so you don't miss your target. Be sure he understands that he is not to move or take his hands off the chair until you are finished, and then only when you give him permission. Let him know that if he disobeys, he will receive another swat. If he still moves after the first swat, don't wrestle with him. Go back to square one and start over. Outlast until he submits *properly* to one or two single swats.

Give one swat at a time with a pause in between. Be patient and don't rush. A spanking should be a calm, controlled affair, not a wild free-for-all. Usually only a relatively short period of time, and only a total of two or three swats, will be required before a resisting child gives in and obeys. If this is the first time you've tried this, it will take longer.

Stop when he is submitting properly. If you give too many swats, or give them too rapidly, he will be far more likely to keep resisting. Don't engage in a wrestling match when spanking.

> *He is on the path of life who heeds instruction, but he who forsakes reproof goes astray.*
>
> *- Proverbs 10:17*

## The Key to Spanking Seldom, Not Often

**Magda:** You say you rarely spank. I appreciate this. Unfortunately, I seem to spank all the time. I've been trying to cut back, but haven't figured out how, since my children are extremely rambunctious and always getting into something. What should I do?

**Elizabeth:** Your inquiry suggests to me that your children have picked up on ways to get around you and are getting away with numerous little things without your realizing it. I suspect that you are giving them too much freedom and expecting too little of them. Are you allowing too much rowdiness "because they are children"? Little children do not need to be "extremely rambunctious." It's time to raise your standards, disallowing all wild behavior. Start correcting *before* things get out of control. The key to decreasing spanking incidents is vigilance, consistency, and nipping things in the bud.

*Do not hold back discipline from the child...*

*- Proverbs 23:13*

## Disciplining in Public

**Joany:** I hate to spank my child in public even though he may need it. How can I avoid correcting in public, yet be consistent and correct every time?

**Elizabeth:** I agree with your reluctance to discipline in public. If you can't discipline the instant your child misbehaves (in a restaurant, for example), consider using one of the following strategies:

1. **Minimize the damage, then work on further training after returning home.** For the youngest toddlers, distract or pacify them until you are able to leave the scene. Once home, I rarely discipline very young children because they cannot make the connection between cause and effect when you wait any period of time. I don't simply dismiss the matter, however.

Public misbehavior signals to me that I have done an insufficient job training them, and I need to be far more vigilant in the future. So from then on, I look for similar character problems at home and train there. Thorough training at home is by far the best way to avoid embarrassment when you are out in public.

2. **Leave the scene immediately and discipline in the car or at home.** If the child is old enough to benefit from an after-the-fact spanking, then I might leave for home and discipline as soon as possible. I have only very rarely done this. Again, I am more inclined to defer discipline at that particular time and begin closer Tomato Staking and retraining at home. Be assured that whatever the problem was, it will surface again. Watch for similar behavior at home (setting up tempting situations, if needed) and correct emphatically and consistently there.

3. **"Count" each infraction and discipline accordingly when you get home.** One of my favorite ways of handling public misbehavior is to "count." Here's how it works: Suppose I am going shopping with a few young children. I pause outside the store to go over my behavior expectations with them, "Don't touch, talk softly, stay beside me, and don't ask for anything." While I'm at it, I also explain to them that if they disobey I am going to "count," adding one "count" for each disobedience. Once we are home, each child will receive a swat with the paddle, for each "count" he racked up.

This counting method works wonders with children old enough to appreciate after-the-fact discipline. I've never gotten past the count of three before they've taken it to heart and shaped up. (And once they understand the process, it also works great for misbehavior in the car, when Mom is driving and unable to correct in any other way.)

In all three of the above cases, employ immediate Tomato Staking to keep things under control until you are home. Continue Tomato Staking *after* you are home and after you've applied whatever discipline you may have felt necessary. Think "retraining," not "punishment." This is more important than anything else.

*Do not reprove a scoffer, lest he hate you, reprove a wise man, and he will love you.*

*- Proverbs 9:8*

## Spanking Teens

**Mason:** I attended a strict Christian school where even the high school seniors were severely paddled for minor offenses. I deeply resent it to this day. Is this the kind of discipline you advocate?

**Elizabeth:** No, I don't advocate spanking teenagers, and certainly not for trivial offenses. Spanking is a training mechanism that instills in toddlers and young children respect and obedience. Occasionally, spanking may be needed with grade-school-aged children—usually those not trained to obey when younger, or those who are having behavior problems due to outside influences.

Rebellious teens are generally beyond the point where a spanking is effective anyway, and all it does is cause bitterness. Occasionally I do receive a testimony from someone who tells me that they were spanked as a teen, on a particular occasion, for a particular major offense, and it turned them around. They are very grateful. But those are one-time special circumstances, not the use of spanking as routine teen discipline, such as you seem to have experienced.

Removal of privileges and negative outside influences, along with intensive Tomato Staking and lots of communication, is a far better way to deal with teens than spanking.

*He whose ear listens to the life-giving reproof will dwell among the wise.*

*- Proverbs 15:31*

## Options Other Than Spanking

**Jewels:** Are there any effective discipline options besides spanking? I ask because I grew up in a severely dysfunctional family where physical, mental, and alcohol abuse were daily occurrences. The times I have tried spanking have left me emotionally devastated. Counseling has put my life back on track, but I'm simply unable, emotionally, to administer a spanking. Any help?

**Elizabeth:** Several parents have asked me how to discipline without spanking. Some, like you, find spanking traumatic. Others have foster children who cannot by law be spanked. Some live in countries where spanking is actually illegal. If, for whatever reason, you *can't* spank, you can still use "Tomato Staking," outlasting, ambushing, and standing in the corner. When spanking is left out, these approaches are often much harder to apply, but they will work if you are extremely diligent. (Spanking, if done correctly, just accelerates the process and makes it less emotionally taxing on both the parent and child.)

If you are training a small child who refuses your order, you can skip the spanking, but you still must stop him from doing anything else until he obeys you. Keep his attention, and keep telling him what you expect, until he obeys. This outlasting often seems to last forever, but it is an effective, proven option to spanking.

Ambushing is also harder without the spanking option. You have to watch twice as vigilantly, and catch misbehavior twice as promptly. Instead of spanking, you might immediately banish the child to the corner, keeping him there until he is very bored and motivated to obey you. You must watch vigilantly when you release him. You must be ready to promptly apply the same strict discipline for every single infraction. Without the spanking option, much tight, lengthy Tomato Staking is usually required. You may use other forms of discipline, but in order for them to work, extreme consistency will be mandatory.

> *For they our earthly fathers disciplined us for a short time as seemed best to them..., but He disciplines us for our good, that we may share His holiness.*
>
> *- Hebrews 12:10*

## Each Unique Child

When it comes to spanking or any other discipline tool, it is critical that each child be treated differently according to his own uniqueness. If you start with a young child and the very mild training swats described earlier, you will learn very quickly whether to apply more firmness or less. A stern look, or a simple "Don't do that again," may work very well for one child, while a persuasive spanking might be necessary with another.

Yet another might respond best to standing in a corner or sitting next to you for awhile. Others, who are strong-willed or impetuous, may simply require a longer period of consistent Tomato Staking. What one child learns in a day, may take another child several months to learn. Expect these differences between children and adjust your discipline methods accordingly.

The inflexible prerequisite is this: know your own children. Discipline only to the point of sincere repentance and no more. Always aim at the same result—obedience with a good attitude—but get to that point by being creative and flexible, altering good methods and techniques according to personality, age, and circumstance.

If you don't need to spank, then don't spank. But beware of falling into the easy trap of using impoverished methods such as yelling, nagging, shaming, bribing and manipulating. These are much harder on a child than a simple spanking and can create lifelong negative repercussions.

**NOTE:** Even if you initially do spank, once your child has learned to respect you, you should no longer need to spank. Except on very rare occasions, a verbal rebuke or another mild form of discipline should be sufficient. In all cases, Tomato Staking is extremely helpful.

*He who neglects discipline despises himself, but he who listens to reproof acquires understanding.*

*- Proverbs 15:32*

# Part III

# Emotional Issues

*Whenever I get discouraged, I take a look at my older daughters who were not trained this way and know I'm doing the right thing with Teresa! I'm so glad to have found this website when I did. Thanks Elizabeth for sharing everything you know! I'm sure I would have had brat number three and soon-to-be brat number four if I hadn't found your website. I had no clue what I was doing as a parent. I was trying to raise my kids according to the early education course techniques learned in college. Believe me, wishy-washy discipline does NOT work.*

***Linda***

# nine

# DEALING WITH FEELINGS

*"For out of the heart come evil thoughts, murders, adulteries, fornications, thefts, false witness, slanders."*
*- Matthew 15:19*

## Testimony From an Unrestrained Mom

*Dear Elizabeth,*

*I can personally relate to children whose parents extended them endless permissions and the right to freely express every emotion. Sadly, that's how I grew up. Now, as a Christian adult, I realize how unbiblical it is to habitually "feel any way you happen to feel." It is a very dangerous pattern that may require a lifetime to undo. I am now in my thirties and I continue to battle with self-control, particularly when life gets stressful, and old temptations and bad habits reassert themselves. Thank God for His ever-available grace and help in times of trouble. And thank God my children know the blessings of loving discipline and do not have to grow up the same way I did.*

*Sincerely,*
*Lillian*

Fifty years ago, few parenting authors would have even thought to mention the subject of emotions and whether a child should be taught to control them. It would have been taken for granted. All children were expected to restrain and direct their emotions appropriately, from an early age.

Alas, upon the arrival of psychologists to the field of parenting, common sense in this regard has vanished and we now have an entire generation of young parents who believe their children will be scarred for life if required to manage their spirits.

The results, predictably, are millions of children well on their way to becoming emotional cripples, unable to handle the slightest disappointment or the smallest offense made against them. Many of their similarly-raised parents are in this state already. Perhaps the psychologists have discovered a guaranteed source of fees and new patients.

> *Rescue me, and deliver me out of the hand of aliens, whose mouth speaks deceit, and whose right hand is a right hand of falsehood.*
>
> *- Psalms 144:11*

## Not All Emotions Are Good

It is not wrong to have emotions, but unbridled emotions are dangerous and potentially devastating. Adults who feel righteous indignation upon seeing the innocent suffer, or children who grieve the loss of a grandparent, act properly and nobly. But not all emotions, displayed freely, are good. Both the adult who loses his temper when frustrated, and the child who throws a fit to get his way, are equally reprehensible. Emotions are attributes of God Himself, engendered in us when He "created man in His own image." The challenge is not to eliminate emotions, but to manage them in ways pleasing to God and in accordance with His image.

Because God is gracious, He helps us in this task of becoming like Him—by revealing to us in His Word *when* we are to feel certain emotions and to *what extent*. We are to "hate" evil, for example. We are to "be miserable and mourn and weep" over our own sins. We are to "rejoice" in Him. We are to "love" our neighbor. And so on. In addition to His direct instructions, God offers His example, so that we might imitate Him. Thus, when Exodus tells us that God is "slow to anger," we too must be slow to anger. When the Psalms describe Him as "compassionate and longsuffering," we are to seek to be the same.

Jesus is, of course, our supreme example. His emotional repertoire was vast and we are given many examples thereof. Jesus was "consumed with zeal" when He saw God's house being misused. He "felt compassion" for the lost and taught them, and for the sick, he offered healing. He "wept" when His dear friend Lazarus died. His soul was "deeply grieved" when He prayed in the Garden. And ultimately, Jesus demonstrated "love" beyond compare by laying down His very life for our sakes. In all that He did, He set an example for us to follow and gave us the power to do so.

Along with the biblical descriptions of wisely managed emotions, the Bible also gives us many examples of mismanaged and unrestrained emotions, beginning with Cain, who murdered his own brother in anger, to Moses, who lost his temper and struck the rock, to the malice of the Jewish leaders, who put the Son of God to death. Never are these displays excused because the perpetrators did not have the ability to control their tempers. Apparently God felt they did.

In the next few chapters, I am going to discuss emotions as they relate to parenting small children and how, in practical ways, we can help our children become masters of their own spirits and hence live the rest of their lives free from the bonds of emotional slavery.

*Then the LORD passed by in front of him and proclaimed, "The LORD, the LORD God, compassionate and gracious, slow to anger, and abounding in lovingkindness and truth."*

*- Exodus 34:6*

## You CAN Change Your Emotions

Yes, you CAN change your emotions. You are not a helpless victim of hurt feelings, irritability, and anger. We can and must learn to alter our tempers and deny our feelings, when necessary, and teach our children to do likewise.

*Colossians 3:8* tells us: *"...put them all aside: anger, wrath, malice, slander, and abusive speech from your mouth."* Since here and many places elsewhere in Scripture we are commanded to control our emotions, it's safe to assume God gives us the ability to do so. God tells us what to do, and empowers us to do it, so all we need to do is obey Him. In the same way, we have the ability to teach our children to control their emotions. All they need to do is obey us, as we wisely discipline them and train them according to God's Word.

*"For this commandment which I command you today is not too difficult for you, nor is it out of reach."*

*- Deuteronomy 30:11*

## The Outside Reflects the Inside

One cherished, but highly erroneous modern belief is that a parent should not correct a child for displaying a wrong emotion, because the child will "suppress" the emotion rather than change it. Experience convinces me otherwise. Require young children to display the right emotions outwardly and their hearts will change, producing the right attitudes and emotions inwardly as well.

Of course, you can't simply order your children to "be happy." If the child is small, it works much better to tell him to "smile" or "straighten up your face." If the child is very young, I'll cheerfully say, "Let's see a smile now," or "Where is your smile?"

The child may initially resist, but when he finally obeys, the resulting smile will often break into a radiant grin, accompanied by sincere laughter and other expressions of genuine joy. It is hard for a small child to hide his true feelings. It is equally difficult for him to display an emotion that he does not really feel. Get him to smile on the outside and invariably he will smile on the inside.

*A joyful heart makes a cheerful face, but when the heart is sad,*
*the spirit is broken.*

*- Proverbs 15:13*

## The Photo Shoot

One December several years ago, during our annual family Christmas photo session, the task of arranging and making twelve people presentable was proving a taxing experience. After an hour and at least fifty shots, our four-year-old commenced pouting and looking miserable. There was talk of surrendering and trying again the next day, but I was thinking, *"NO WAY am I going to go through all this again tomorrow!"*

So I said, "Jeffy, look at me." He looked. I said, "Why are you crying?" He answered, "Because I'm tired." I pleasantly replied, "Do you want to ruin the picture with your crying face?" He paused, then said, "No," as though he hadn't thought of that. I wiped away the tears and said, "Now let's see you smile. Do your funny Donald Duck face, only not all the way, but just a little bit—there, that's it! You look very nice now!"

By this time, Jeffy was almost starting to giggle and I had to restrain the cheer lest his laughing ruin more pictures! The picture we selected told the story: his whole attitude was transformed and he was radiant the rest of the session.

*A joyful heart is good medicine, but a broken spirit dries up the bones.*

*- Proverbs 17:22*

## Changing Thoughts Will Change Emotions

Emotions are a reaction. So what are they a reaction to? Many would say that they are a reaction to a circumstance, but that is really not the case. They are actually a reaction to your *thoughts* about a circumstance. For example, if you can't swim, and you fall into the deep end of the pool, you'll most likely react with terror and panic because your mind will be screaming: *"I CAN'T SWIM! I'M GOING TO DROWN!"* On the other hand, if you are a good swimmer, and fall in the deep end of the same pool, you won't panic. You'll think: *"What a bother! Now I'm soaked; I'd better swim over to the side, get out, and dry off."*

The same analogy can be broadly applied. The body, when surprised, releases a rush of adrenaline, but immediately one's thoughts will influence the extent of the emotional reaction. One may be unable to control the emotions directly, but one *can* control thoughts, and hence emotions produced through them.

By *nature,* I am a somewhat emotional, nervous person. I often have to restrain these feelings lest they get the best of me. I do fine if I can conjure up the right thoughts—the right outlook or perspective—on whatever the situation happens to be. I struggle when I dwell on my fears and other wrong thoughts, or if I am not disciplining myself to believe the thoughts I know are right ones.

I also find that if I allow wrong emotions to rule for even a second or two, it is much harder to get those emotions back under control. Once that adrenaline is flowing, it takes a few minutes to get it out of the system. Still, I can certainly control my voice and large motor skills, and so I do. I attempt as much as possible to always display godly emotions and attitudes on the outside, as I work to change my thinking and the resulting feelings, on the inside.

This is my aim—and what I want to help my children to learn to do as well.

> *...taking every thought captive to the obedience of Christ...*
> *- II Corinthians 10:5*

## Emotion-Changing Tips

When your child is unhappy, do not cajole him into smiling. A smile is easy to elicit if someone is there to baby, comfort, and bribe you into cheer, but that does nothing to raise an emotionally responsible child. What you really seek is a child who believes it is wrong to be a sourpuss, or angry, or fearful, or irritable, and is willing and able on his own to change his outlook. Make it easy for him by smiling yourself and encouraging him. But don't go overboard trying to keep him happy by becoming his personal jester.

Some children are masters of the art of manipulation, getting their way by crying, pouting, or whining. Some think it's their right to become angry over anything that doesn't go their way. To stop this, you must convince them that such behavior will earn from you a response they are certain NOT to enjoy. Be sure your response is swift and unmistakably negative. Once they've submitted to you, move on to teaching them to think godly thoughts instead of their own selfish ones. Not only will they be learning how to restrain wrong emotions, but also how to alter wrong emotions to right ones.

As with all other misbehavior, nipping things in the bud is most productive. Practice observing your children. Learn to read their minds and anticipate their acts and motives. Many parents lament over children who talk back, roll their eyes, refuse to obey quickly, or show other signs of wrong thoughts and emotions. These are the signals you should be looking for. Notice the first indication of a wrong spirit and immediately bring it to your child's attention in order to fix it. If detected early, a simple verbal reminder and perhaps a little coaching about right thoughts should suffice. Allowing an ungodly spirit to take root is your guarantee of far more serious and difficult offenses to follow. Wrong emotions lead to wrong attitudes, and finally to wrong actions.

> *The north wind brings forth rain, and a backbiting tongue, an angry countenance.*
>
> *- Proverbs 25:23*

## The Bethany Story

My otherwise almost perfect second daughter had one very bad habit when she was little. Once a week our family would take a lengthy car trip, arriving home late at night. Each time, just as our car turned into the driveway, she would commence wailing. Telling her to stop, reasoning with her, and even spanking all proved futile. This persisted, week after week. She didn't care if she got spanked or not, as long as she got to cry for a few minutes and upset everyone. Clearly, she liked the frustration and consternation she was causing in the rest of us, as she indulged in her little drama.

Finally, I had enough. The next time, just *before* we turned in the driveway, I turned and watched her face, ready and waiting, with a new plan in place. I popped her seat belt and ambushed her with a firm "I Mean Business" spanking the *split second* she began puckering up her mouth. My lightning-quick response shocked her. She had not even managed to get one peep out yet. She was certainly startled and perhaps even a bit frightened by my no-nonsense, zero-tolerance approach. She had expected to at least get in a little crying before I clamped down on her. Instead, I had deprived her of the smallest scrap of pleasure and induced a measure of discomfort and respect for her mother instead.

She never tried it again. No more crying and carrying on and succumbing to her "feelings" upon arriving home. Just a pleasant, normal child like the rest of her siblings. My hyper ambush had motivated her to change her actions, and along with it, her attitude about arriving home.

Bethany is now an adult and tells me that although she was probably only three or four years old at the time, she remembers the incident, recalling vividly that I finally meant business, and she knew that it was time to straighten up. She laughs when we talk about this story and strongly agrees that I acted appropriately.

> *Let your father and your mother be glad, and let her rejoice who gave birth to you.*
>
> *- Proverbs 23:25*

## Persuade Him Toward Good

**Sandra:** I spank for disobedience and disrespect and know that this can change a child's heart. But one can't always control the inside by spanking. Despite outward compliance, feelings might still be there. Isn't it dangerous to ignore suppressed feelings, taking the risk that the child will become bitter? Instead, wouldn't it be preferable to focus on the need to understand our feelings and deal with them correctly?

**Elizabeth:** Destructive displays of emotions, such as yelling, screaming, crying, self-pity, pouting, and hitting require immediate correction. But you are correct to say that the parent should not stop there, but proceed to address their child's heart. Those whose continual focus is their child's *heart* need not worry about him "suppressing" his feelings. A heart-focused parent will continue to draw out of his child his true inward beliefs and work with them until the child is persuaded toward God and toward good.

Suppose your child hits his sibling. It is not enough to correct only for the hitting; you must also correct the anger that led to the hitting. In virtually no instance is anger toward a sibling justified. If he is not angry, he will not hit. If he is angry, his response will depend on how you've raised him.

Whether he hits or not, if he remains angry, he will likely express his anger at a later time. That is the danger in not addressing the heart. Therefore, to raise a godly child, you must correct the anger in such a way that you eliminate it. Focus on the action first, but then immediately address the inner motivating spirit and be sure it has been changed to a good one.

Because older children are adept at hiding their thoughts and emotions and faking the response you desire to see, you must go farther than simple discipline with them. The older the child, the more words can be used to teach and correct. Address his wrong attitude by verbally teaching him what he should be "thinking" in order to have the *right* attitude.

Discuss what happened and show him what the right response should have been. Coach him on the godly thoughts that should characterize future attitudes and motives. Persuade your child to believe as you do, that we should always strive for godliness in every situation and never be dominated by our feelings.

Verbal instruction like this works especially well in older children who have a personal relationship with Christ and a desire to do His will. But it will also work with any child whose conscience has not been hardened by habitual rebellion and disobedience. Adjust your speech according to the age of the child, then talk, persuade, convince, and talk some more until your child embraces what is good and right.

*Poverty and shame will come to him who neglects discipline,*
*but he who regards reproof will be honored.*
*- Proverbs 13:18*

## No Emotions Allowed?

**Farrah:** I am uncertain about all of this. Do we punish our children for feeling sad, disappointed, or angry? Perhaps I am misunderstanding you, but on your website, you cited a ten-year-old boy who cried for an hour because his party gift was accidentally forgotten at home and he was left empty-handed when everyone else opened their gifts. Yes, he should have stopped crying sooner after receiving comfort and sympathy, but can't we allow them to express any feelings of hurt and disappointment? Are such feelings to be stifled and suppressed? How should the situation have been handled?

**Elizabeth:** In the story you cited, the child was old enough to understand why his gift was missing, and that he'd get it later. He was also old enough to act graciously, despite his disappointment, and to enjoy the party, even without his gift. He understood all of this and deliberately chose to dramatize his disappointment and demand attention. The child cried and carried on far too long, ruining the party for everyone. His reaction was excessive and his motivation was self-centered.

Let's analyze the boy's thought processes and discuss how the mom should have handled him. When he realized he wasn't getting a present, he probably thought: *"Woe is me; instead of something special, I'm getting nothing. Woe is me; everyone else is getting a present and having fun but me."* If a child is given too much sympathy and thus encouraged to indulge such thinking, he will very likely become more angry and self-centered as he contemplates all the reasons he has to justify his unhappiness.

It's a short step to the next descending stage of self-pity and rage: *"I never get any presents. When I do, they are not as nice as everyone else's. Mom doesn't care, so I don't think I'll give her a hug. She's mean to me. She likes everyone else better than she does me…."*

Instead of continuing to sympathize and console him, after allowing a short reasonable period of disappointment, the mom should have stopped the child and initiated a session in coaching and training: "Jimmy, look at me. Stop crying. Good, now listen to me. Jimmy, you know that I always do my best to get you a nice gift. You know that it was an accident that your gift was forgotten at home. Now, put a smile on your face and enjoy the party and everyone else's gifts until you get home. Find a way to make everyone else happy today, not just yourself. Good. That's better! Smile and think about pleasing the others right now. You will get your gift later."

A child in the habit of expressing unrestrained emotions or being self-centered may need more persistent, determined lecturing, and perhaps even a little discipline in cases like this. The most important step is to stop the bad thoughts before they escalate, and replace them with good ones.

You should not attempt to stifle or suppress your child's feelings, but rather than allowing him to indulge his emotions, it is far better for your child to teach him the appropriate response to disappointment and other hurts or frustrations. Teach him to control his spirit and choose to think right and good thoughts.

*Train up a child in the way he should go, even when he is old he will not depart from it.*

*- Proverbs 22:6*

## Clunked on the Head

**Rebecca:** What if a child has a good reason to get upset? Suppose your child was intentionally struck on the head with a block. Shouldn't you just tell your child, "It is okay to be mad, but you need to get over it. Don't be too offended and go forgive your little brother who clunked you"?

**Elizabeth:** Despite provocation, it's never acceptable to be mad when offended. We are supposed to be imitating Christ, and Christ patiently endured suffering and overcame evil with good. Christ taught us to "turn the other cheek" and to "go the extra mile." So no, I would never tell my child that it was "okay to be mad."

I'd react to the overt aggression in your story by immediately reprimanding and disciplining the offending child. The next step would be expressing concern and sympathy briefly to the wounded child, then spending whatever time was needed to help him think rightly and display good character. I would tell him to stop crying, then give him better thoughts to think: "Your little brother needs to learn not to throw things. I'm glad you didn't get angry and throw something back at him. If he ever starts acting like that again, come and get me so I can correct him." It would also be wise to make the guilty child apologize and the victim accept the apology.

Let's suppose the victim did indeed become angry and launched a return attack on the instigator. In that case, I would discipline both children. The perpetrator would be disciplined the most severely of the two, but the victim would also be corrected for retaliating. I would have to assess the spirits of both carefully and correct them according to what they did and their responses to my reprimands. **I would *not* be discussing emotions,** which will only increase their self-centeredness. I would direct the focus onto actions and how to have right thoughts.

> *A man's discretion makes him slow to anger, and it is his glory to overlook a transgression.*
>
> *- Proverbs 19:11*

## Desensitizing the Emotional Child

Some children are highly sensitive, emotional, or depressed, precisely *because* their parents have encouraged them to believe they have no power or control over their emotions. I'd be depressed too if I believed there was no hope that I could ever feel any differently—if I believed I would be the captive of my feelings for the rest of my life.

A more naturally "sensitive" or "emotional" child needs *extra* help learning to control his emotions, not a free pass to let them run (and ruin) his life. This means that Mom must make a special effort to teach and train a child like this to control and change his wrong emotions and express his right ones appropriately. Several of my children are naturally sensitive, and the more I sympathized with them or allowed free emotional expression when they were little, the worse they became. On the other hand, they improved greatly when I reined them in and taught them to control their emotions.

I did that by first requiring them to control the outward show of those emotions when they were inappropriate—crying over minor issues, for example. Then I taught them to think more godly thoughts and to help them develop the right attitude and hence, emotions. Today, no one would believe that these same children were once ultra-sensitive.

> *A tranquil heart is life to the body, but passion is rottenness to the bones.*
>
> *- Proverbs 14:30*

## The Fearful Child

**Glenda:** My five-year-old son is terrified of spiders and refused to come downstairs this morning because there was a tiny spider on the steps. He sobbed and carried on. Since the bug was too small for me to see, I told *him* to vacuum it up, but he would not. I don't think it was an obedience issue; I think he was simply too terrified to obey.

I had no idea how to handle the situation. Should I have disciplined him, or hugged and comforted him? How can we possibly go camping this summer, if he is going to erupt at the sight of a spider? Thanks in advance.

**Elizabeth:** First, never discipline or "punish" a child for having true fears. Likewise, avoid, if at all possible, forcing a child to do what he is sincerely afraid to do. Don't encourage his fears by "comforting" an excessively frightened child either, saying, "It's okay to be afraid of spiders Honey; come and let Mummy give you a big hug."

What you need to do is WORK WITH the child to help eradicate his fears. My own approach is to be honest and matter-of-fact: "Son, stop crying. It's only a spider. God made them, and they make beautiful webs no one could ever duplicate. They are useful in the garden, and they are not going to hurt you. Who is bigger? You or that spider? I bet that spider is more afraid of you than you are of him. Now let me show you how to get rid of a spider...." Remember that the child's fear is irrational. If you deal calmly and reassuringly with his fear, you will give him confidence and the problem will quickly subside.

> *Do not fear, for I am with you; do not anxiously look about you, for I am your God. I will strengthen you, surely I will help you, surely I will uphold you with My righteous right hand.*
>
> *- Isaiah 41:10*

## Getting Tough on Emotionalism

**Lisa:** Today as my boys were playing Playmobil, I joined in. I picked up a Playmobil man from the floor and took it to my four-year-old across the room. He *immediately* started to cry. I had no idea why. He said he "was using that guy." I replied, "no you weren't; it was lying on the floor." Then he crossed his arms on his chest and in an angry voice said, "Now I have zero guys, so I can't play!"

I told him to stop, that it was nothing to cry over. If he had simply *asked* for the man instead of getting angry, I would have given it to him. But he kept on crying. I spanked him, only to hear him whisper to himself, "I am very, very, very angry!" I talked to him, yet he persisted in his pouting and anger.

What did I do wrong? I am finding myself getting angry and frustrated, because this is becoming a habitual reaction. HELP!

**Elizabeth:** Had it been me, I think that when I realized that reasoning was futile, I would have quit the reasoning, ordered him to knock it off, and then commenced to discipline and outlast as needed to change his self-centered attitude. He could go back to playing once he was thankful that he had the toy at all and was happy to share it.

**Followup from Lisa:** Dear Elizabeth, Hallelujah! My four-year-old no longer pouts…at all! I cannot remember his last bout, but it was around the time I wrote to you about the Playmobil "guy" incident. What you suggested worked! Now he is much happier, does not pout, whine, complain…EVER! Your biblically-based advice works, and WOW…our home is so much happier and peaceful now compared to a year ago. THANK YOU!

*Stern discipline is for him who forsakes the way….*
*- Proverbs 15:10*

## Fixing the Meltdown

**Heidi:** My three-year-old has a whining and crying problem we have been unable to solve. Her response to every directive is to dissolve into tears. I treat this as a mild temper tantrum and spank her. The effect is more tears and louder cries.

After a pause, I tell her with a smile: "Stop crying and let me see your happy face." She will try to smile, offer a fake grin, all the while struggling to suppress her sobbing. I will say, "Good!" and give her a big happy mommy smile.

Then she will go and do whatever I told her, but as she walks off, she'll start crying again. I will call her back, swat her, and tell her to "get happy." The whole cycle repeats itself over and over. How do you get a child to stop crying over a spanking and get REALLY happy, not just until Mom's back is turned?

**Elizabeth:** If a justified spanking produces tears, allow a *short* reasonable amount of time for the child to collect himself and stop. Only spank again if the crying increases, becomes exaggerated, or expresses anger toward you for the spanking. That angry type of crying warrants another spanking, but never *keep* spanking a child. Spank (one or two swats) then pause and give the child time to decide if he wants to comply, or keep rebelling with rage against your rightful authority. Outlast.

If your child is simply in the habit of crying over every trifle, be watching for the first signs and stop it before it leads to a major meltdown. It helps to warn this type of child when you first give your instructions: "Sally, come here. I'm going to ask you do something and I want you to do it cheerfully, with a smile on your face. If you cannot do it cheerfully, you will have to stand in the corner until you can. Do you understand? Good. Let's try it...."

With habitual weepers, it is best to avoid spanking for this. Send them immediately and consistently to the corner instead.

> *Everyone who is proud in heart is an abomination to the LORD; Assuredly, he will not be unpunished.*
> *- Proverbs 16:5*

## Waking Up on the Wrong Side of the Bed

Before I get into more questions and answers about the emotional displays of crying and whining, I'd like to relate one more simple story about how excessive emotionalism was handled in our house.

When my oldest was small, he used to wake up every morning and come downstairs crying and whining about something trivial. A typical example would be, "Whaaaaa, my pillow fell on the floor." Funny at first, it became old in a hurry. One day, he appeared wearing his whining face, and I decided to stop it. I looked at him and said, "Now go back upstairs, and don't come down until you can name three things you are thankful for today." He was surprised, but obeyed. A little later, he came down and listed three things he was thankful for. I had him repeat this exercise every morning for a week. The crying game was over, never to reappear.

Discipline for crying does not always have to be a spanking. Get creative and come up with something that motivates your child, that can be applied immediately, and that addresses the heart.

> *Do all things without grumbling or disputing.*
>
> *- Philippians 2:14*

# ten

# CRYING AND WHINING

*Therefore now, O LORD, please take my life from me, for death is better to me than life.*
*- Jonah 4:3*

## Types of Crying

One of the natural symptoms of the emotionalism discussed in the previous chapter is crying. Everyone has had their patience tested by a child who whines and cries. It requires a discerning parent to know why a child is crying and apply the proper remedy. To ease matters, I'm offering the following examples of several types of crying and how you might respond:

1. **The "lonely" child:** A child starved for his mother's attention may react by whining. Being constantly critical or aloof with your child may produce the same response. Give a child like this more of your love and attention. Remember to keep him with you and let him help you whenever possible. Look for things to encourage, rather than infractions to criticize. A renewed display of interest on your part will restore his sense of security, and your sad child will turn into a cheerful, confident one in short order. Try to ignore the initial whining and continue to give more attention in the future.

2. **The "tired or sick" child:** If your child exhibits an unusual increase in whining, examine the circumstances. Could he be ill? Does he have a temperature? Did he get enough sleep last night? Has he eaten lately? If you find something amiss, treat the problem as needed and overlook the whining. If it is a matter of weariness, you can always have your child lie down beside you and take a little nap. Don't let this go too far though. Despite fatigue, a child should *still* be expected to obey simple directions with a cooperative spirit. A deferred nap is no excuse for him to inflict misery on everyone around him. Correct him for any misbehavior as always, but provide for his needs by seeing that he gets more sleep.

3. **The "sensitive" child:** Although all children are different and some are indeed more "sensitive" than others, I'm convinced that parents often inadvertently encourage hypersensitivity by overreacting to minor injuries or by extending too much sympathy when their child suffers minor slights. In these cases, parents need to alter their own responses if they hope to effect change in their child. Remember, children will imitate your reactions to different situations and will pick up both good and bad attitudes from you. If you become hysterical when a minor injury occurs, expect the same from your child. If you are always feeling mistreated, your child will too.

My children sometimes rush to me crying over an invisible bump or scratch. I examine the spot seriously and then offer my smiling assessment: "I think you'll live." I grin, tussle their hair, and give a comforting hug. I may ask in a mock-serious tone if we should call the ambulance for a trip to the hospital. (They never want that.) Sometimes I tell them, with a smile, "Well, I don't see any blood, so I think you're all right." Then I send them back to what they were doing or engage them in some other pleasant activity.

If the child has hurt *feelings,* I shift the focus to teaching him a more appropriate way to think, feel, and respond. I talk to him and encourage him to be nice to the other person anyway. We consider together some of the reasons why the offender might have acted that way. This creates the understanding that renders the act of forgiveness easier. I encourage him not to be easily offended and hurt by the actions or words of others. The objective here is to desensitize the overly sensitive child. A side benefit will be less crying.

4. **Crying due to "injury":** Obviously you must find out if your child is really hurt or not. If there is an injury, but it's not too serious, I will tell my child, "It's okay; we'll just clean this up and take care of it." I treat injuries matter-of-factly, not with hysterical panic or with too much indulgent sympathy.

If an injury is serious, apply first aid and head for the emergency room. GIVE COMFORT; IGNORE CRYING. If truly injured, a child's crying will often subside once he's been comforted and attended to. If he continues to cry unnecessarily, encourage him to stop with a calm and simple, "That's enough crying now." If your child is trained to obey, he will stop. If he isn't, and doesn't stop, don't use this as a training session. There are more appropriate times and opportunities for that.

5. **Very minor injury; crying for sympathy:** Toddlers cry at the drop of a hat for the smallest injury. It's a natural way for them to communicate and the urge doesn't disappear overnight with the acquisition of a few words.

But as they grow older, it's the parents' job to teach them to control this urge to cry over everything. Some crying is legitimate and tolerable—when the dog dies, or when you suffer a real injury. But it's not permissible to cry when you don't get what you want or when Mom says "no." Crying over such trifles as these has nothing to do with pain or suffering, but is rather a demand for attention and sympathy. That being the case, do not commiserate with him any more than necessary. Doing so will encourage his continued self-pity and will likely even escalate the crying. Teach your child that it's okay to cry for a minute or so, but not for too long. Point out to him that if he cries long and loud over minor things, no one will listen when he is *really* hurt.

6. **Manipulative crying and whining:** This is the kind of crying that many otherwise well-behaved children soon discover and use against you for as long as you will let them. Too compliant to defy you outright, they have no qualms about passively manipulating you with their tears and sad faces.

Usually it starts with a true injury or emotional hurt. They cry and receive attention, as they should. But then one day, they realize just how much they enjoy this type of attention. A few seconds later, it occurs to them that they can very easily obtain more by more crying and whining. The next step is the discovery that they can get their way in all sorts of matters, once again, by more crying and whining. Soon they are employing this mechanism to rule the home.

Be honest in your assessment of your child to discern whether he is crying to manipulate or not. If he is, you can only stop it by being prompt, rigorous, and relentless. Begin by stating there will be no more unprovoked crying, no more crying when Mom says "no," and no more crying for minor injuries. Then, prepare to be a mean mother. Stand him in the corner or even spank, IMMEDIATELY, with the first sniffle. Whatever you do, you must discipline EVERY TIME without exception. If he tones down the crying, but switches to pouting and sniffling instead, tell him that counts too. Only silence and a pleasant face will do. Be tough and maintain a zero-tolerance approach to such manipulation.

7. **Defiant crying and screaming:** The most disagreeable type of crying is the kind that exhibits bold, angry defiance, and rage. This type of crying should never be allowed to continue. Once he is older, he'll be swearing instead of crying. Two or three "I mean business" swats on the posterior are in order for this type of outburst. The spanking itself may not immediately stop the screaming, but it will communicate your intolerance for this kind of disrespect. To bring him back under control, corner time and

outlasting will likely be needed as well, especially if you did not administer the initial spanking soon enough. Let him go only when he is again calm, quiet, and has composed himself. Be sure he is willing to obey you unconditionally with a pleasant attitude. Then apply close Tomato Staking according to need after that. Never tolerate this type of defiant screaming.

*Strike a scoffer and the naive may become shrewd, but reprove one who has understanding and he will gain knowledge.*
*- Proverbs 19:25*

## Whining Instead of Asking

**Nancy:** My two-year-old can talk, but she whines for whatever she wants, instead of asking. What do I do to stop this?

**Elizabeth:** First, be sure she is obeying you well in other areas. Then, every time she whines for something, tell her to stop whining and ask nicely. If she doesn't stop immediately, view it as a training opportunity.

Tell her to close her mouth and be quiet. Stay close to her and hold her chin up toward you and require her to look at you. Repeat your instructions as needed and outlast, without spanking, until she obeys.

When she is quiet, tell her how she must request things. Demonstrate for her, using the tone of voice you require and the proper words—"Juice please, Mommy?" Have her imitate you. Smile and congratulate her as she tries.

Once she's got it right and is displaying a nice attitude, respond pleasantly and positively. Remind her to "ask nicely like that the next time."

Repeat this process every time she whines. Watch for times when she doesn't whine, but asks correctly, the way you've taught her, and reward her with a bit of praise: "Sure! You may have some juice! And the way you asked so nicely makes me very happy!"

> *"And when they received it, they grumbled at the landowner, saying, 'These last men have worked only one hour, and you have made them equal to us who have borne the burden and the scorching heat of the day.'"*
>
> *- Matthew 20:11-12*

## Screaming When She Doesn't Get Her Way

**Angie:** My nineteen-month-old daughter screams bloody murder when she doesn't get her way. What can I do to stop this?

**Elizabeth:** Because she is young, I'd train her for obedience in other things first. Loud crying or screaming is hard to stop because it is such a spontaneous and automatic emotional reaction. First, train her to obey every other request promptly. Once she knows that she must *always* obey you and does so consistently, it will be much easier to stop the screaming. In fact, it will most likely lessen or even cease on its own. Once taught to respect and obey, she should relent when you simply say, "Stop crying."

Now, assuming that she understands "no," and is beginning to obey, here's what I would do. I would have her look at me and say, "No. Stop screaming." I'd administer a gentle, painless pat on the mouth so she would know what I was referring to.

Screaming is like blinking to a little child. You have to get her to realize that she is doing it, that her mouth is the problem, and that she can control her mouth. Instead of saying, "Be quiet," instruct her to "close" her mouth instead. That makes more sense to a toddler.

Keep your own voice low. Say "Shhhhhh" and hold your finger to your lips. (This will come in handy later when you're in church and can't use your voice.) Pause, then repeat until she stops. Do not allow her to do anything else until she is quiet and ready to obey nicely. Outlast her. Avoid spanking unless she becomes angry.

If she does become angry, stay firm and don't back down. Don't keep patting her mouth. That is just to get the idea across, which should happen very quickly. Switch to giving a firm swat on the bottom now and then if her angry screaming persists. Don't keep swatting either. Just be deliberate and swat occasionally as needed to let her know that you won't relent. Persist until she gives in and is quiet. Outlast her.

If she is determined, this may take a long time, so be prepared and don't try this when you are in a hurry. Once she gives in (or tires out) and stops, give her something else to do that you can control. Sit her next to you for a few minutes before letting her go back to playing.

To get this to stick for the long term, watch her and repeat the process with every relapse. If you do your job, she will eventually be motivated to control herself, and the screaming bouts will be over.

*Do not complain…*

*- James 5:9*

## An Older Child Who Cries to Get His Way

**Ida:** My eight-year-old son has developed a baffling and irritating new habit. Deny him anything he wants and he erupts with a siren-like cry that grows into a sobbing, tearful temper tantrum! I know I shouldn't yield, but I can't stand it and I do. I would like some other way of handling the situation. Any suggestions?

**Elizabeth:** If this is unusual behavior for him, I'd look for something troubling him. Is he having problems with his schoolwork? Have you been unable to give him the usual amount of attention lately? Are there any hidden fears? Address these problems first and give him a little time and see what happens. Meanwhile try to avoid situations that might encourage this behavior.

*But,* if there is no change, or if the misbehavior worsens, get tough. As soon as he starts, discipline him in some way that is *immediate* and *negative*, and makes him regret his misbehavior.

Ignoring never works because we never truly ignore completely. It's impossible to ignore a screaming child forever. At some point, you will show evidence that the crying is having its intended effect, and that's all the child needs to keep him going.

A good primary strategy is to stand him in a corner where he has no audience. Put him where he can't see if you are watching (but be sure you ARE watching), and where there is nothing to divert him. Ignore the crying, but step in and discipline if he turns or leaves the corner or otherwise disobeys. Eventually, he'll get tired of screaming and will stop and ask to come out.

When he does, tell him, "Good, now because you were crying for no reason, you must stand there for a while longer. I'll let you go when you can act like a decent human being." Adding this extra time will make him think twice about doing it again. Do this unfailingly, every time, the instant he starts the crying. Don't speak to him during this corner time, since your attention (even if negative) will reward him and encourage him to continue crying.

Do not express sympathy when he cries to get his way. Explain the new rules: "You whine, you go to the corner." Then stick by them. Don't set a specific limit for the amount of time you keep him in the corner. Don't budge until he has a good attitude, one that expresses remorse and willingness to obey. Do all the "gentle" teaching you wish *after* he has chosen to be quiet and obey.

*When a wise man has a controversy with a foolish man, the foolish man either rages or laughs, and there is no rest.*
*- Proverbs 29:9*

## A Compliant Child Who Whines

**Elaine:** My three-year-old daughter is fairly well behaved except that she whines and pouts. Is there any way to stop this? My husband wants to spank her, but I don't think that will work. Today, I completely ignored an episode and it went away eventually, but to ignore it is not a solution. Is there a better way?

**Elizabeth:** Consider this odd fact: it is invariably the compliant children who do the most whining and pouting. The reason: they can get away with these things without directly defying you. They have a lingering trace of rebellion, but fear the consequences of direct confrontation. So they use this more subtle approach.

It's difficult to discipline these children, because they are usually so good, and Mom feels guilty for getting tough with them over something so seemingly minor. But, of course, if you don't get tough, they will persist. A pessimistic, self-pitying adult is very unattractive.

Ignoring is not the answer. Just as most moms can't bring themselves to spank for whining, neither can they totally ignore whining. So the child picks up on the small signs that show that Mom is annoyed, the child's hopes rise, and the whining increases. The parents become more and more frustrated, and eventually they lash out at the child in anger. Now matters are far worse than they were to begin with. The child is crying instead of whining, and the parents are feeling twice as frustrated and guilty to boot.

Spanking seldom works either, unless you can remain calm, spank briskly at the first sign of whining, and do so religiously upon every occasion. (That works.) Still, most parents have trouble spanking for whining, and I confess that I do too. It just seems too harsh for such a minor infraction. Of course, that's why the whining persists. Whiners know you are not going to get tough with them. Their misbehavior and rebellion has located a perfect safe haven!

So I continue to search for creative, non-spanking options to cure the whiners. I've already detailed the outlasting approach. Sometimes continued reeducation helps: "I will not listen when you are whining and crying. Talk to me in a nice voice." Immediate banishment to the corner is often very effective.

Whatever option you elect, you will succeed only if you nip it in the bud, take all the reward out of it for them, and don't let them do anything else until they stop whining completely and can talk in a normal tone of voice.

*Jesus answered and said to them, "Do not grumble…."*
*- John 6:43*

## "The Screamer"

Here's a helpful exchange between myself and several other moms with regard to their screaming children:

**Tami:** My daughter, almost three, has been a screamer since birth. Although things are improving, she still does it far too often—and she is so LOUD! She will cry over things that are very small and trivial. It's so bad that she's nicknamed "The Screamer" amongst our relatives. Here's an example:

*(She comes to me and asks if she can sit on my lap when I am at the computer.)*
**Me:** "No sweetie."
*(She begins to wail loudly.)*
**Me:** "Stop fussing right now."
*(She cries.)*
**Me:** *(I spank her one swat)* "Stop right now."
*(She cries louder.)*

**Me:** *(I spank again, and then give her a few seconds to compose herself.)*
*(She makes no effort to stop.)*
**Me:** "Stop crying right now."
*(She continues to scream.)*
**Me:** "Look at me. Stop crying—now."

This goes on, with variations, for what seems like forever. She cries; I spank and instruct; she cries; repeat, repeat, repeat. Finally she stops, smiles for me, and obeys my instructions for her to "wait."

But it doesn't end there. A few minutes later she begins howling again and the entire scene repeats itself. It never seems to really end until she either gets what she wants or until her mind wanders off onto some other subject. That is just one instance of what repeats itself throughout the day, every day. Any ideas?

**Elizabeth:** She's got quite a habit going there, doesn't she? Not only is it a habit, but I think she must be getting some satisfaction out of all the attention and drama.

Clearly, what you are doing isn't working. I think you need to try a different approach to break this habitual cycle. As soon as she erupts, say nothing, but administer one firm swat to the bottom and stand her in the corner. Choose a corner where you can see her, but be sure she stays facing the wall so she cannot see any of your inadvertent reactions to her annoying crying. Do not audibly react to her either. It is very important that she does not feel she has an audience.

Don't order her to stop crying yet. Simply let her know that if she wants to cry, she must stand in the corner by herself—"Where I don't have to listen to you." Spank if she leaves the corner, but otherwise pay no attention to her. She'll probably continue to exercise her lungs for a while, but eventually she'll get tired and stop.

Soon she'll ask to leave the corner. Tell her, "No." Don't say anything else. She'll probably start crying again, but ignore her. Only step in if she sits down or tries to leave the corner. Don't say anything, just correct her and return her to the corner. At that point tell her, "You wanted to cry, so stand here and cry. Don't ask when you can leave. I'll tell you when you can leave."

Trust me, she will know why she is there, so don't explain any more than that. The more you talk, the more excuses you'll provide for her to continue arguing with you via her whining, sniffling, and crying.

Eventually, she will be standing quietly. Let her stand for a while longer. This entire process may occupy a half hour or so at first. Even if she gets the idea quickly and cooperates, wait until she is thoroughly bored before releasing her. Don't talk to her or interact with her at all except to correct as needed. When you are certain she has the right attitude (not crying, and resigned to spending the rest of her life in the corner), *then* tell her to come to you. Have her look at you and ask her if she is finished crying. She'll probably say, "Yes." Respond to her with, "Good, now go play and don't let me hear that crying any more."

**Important: Repeat this the next time she starts up again and every time thereafter.**

The idea here is to surprise her with a different approach that gives you several advantages: First, it changes the focus from something you can't easily control (her crying) to something you *can* easily control (standing in the corner). Next, it removes all the pleasure she gets from the crying. (That's why it is important not to visibly or audibly respond to her.) Lastly, standing in the corner is something that will make her uncomfortable and motivate her to give up her beloved screaming habit.

Because you can't really stop her from crying, remember not to *tell* her to stop crying until she is willing to cooperate. That way, she gains no sense of power or satisfaction from continuing to disobey you.

**Tami:** Thank you! I am trying it right this very minute. I hadn't even finished reading your answer when she started a screaming altercation with her sister. I gave her a firm swat, put her in the corner, and told her to stay there. She got quiet pretty quick! She fussed for a second, then put her fingers in her mouth (a habit we only allow at night time). I corrected her and said, "Fingers OUT." Then she cried a little more. So far so good! She has been standing there for about a minute, totally silent. I will update you on how it goes the rest of the day!

**Elizabeth:** Now don't release her too soon. Make sure it soaks in.

**Tami:** Ok, the first time I probably let her go too soon. After I told her, "No fingers," she became quiet and stood still, so I let her go after five minutes. I hope that's okay.

**Tami:** Second time: A bit later she began the same excessive crying again. She was sitting in a box and her baby sister crawled in with her, which launched her into a crying frenzy. I said, "Out of the box, now." I placed her in the corner and said nothing.

She didn't fuss at all. Several times she sighed a little. Then she started playing with her clothes and I told her to stop. She started to cry, but it didn't last long. Overall, she stood there for about fifteen minutes.

**Tami:** Third time: This crying jag is bad. Right before lunch, she hit her big sister. I gave her a swat and said, "No hitting." She cried and cried and cried, so in the corner she went. It's lunchtime now and she is still there. Every few minutes, she senses that she might miss lunch and she starts to scream. She alternates between quiet and screaming, but never stays quiet long enough for me to let her out. I took her to the bathroom for a potty break, after which it was straight back to corner. Finally, after about five minutes of complete silence, I let her out. She is so happy now and being such a sweetie!

**Elizabeth:** Good job so far!

**Tami:** Fourth time: She made it through her lunch and was being as sweet as can be. When she finished, I told her she could have some fruit snacks in a minute. Well, she then started this slight fussing, which isn't full out crying, but just little sobs, if you know what I mean. So I told her, "You need to wait a minute and then you will get them." I sat there and watched her while holding the fruit snacks in my hand. She kept doing her little sobbing thing while trying to pretend she wasn't crying, so I sent her back to the corner. She is there now and it has been fifteen minutes. She is crying off and on. Whenever she stops, it is only because she has her fingers in her mouth. After I tell her to take them out she starts screaming again.

Okay, another five minutes have passed. She has been silent for these five minutes with no fingers in her mouth. I let her out of the corner and again she is so happy and loving. I told her to go color. She asked politely for her fruit snacks after she started to color. I said, "Yes, but you must wait a minute." She said, "Ok mommy, I wait." And she did, very patiently! She was thrilled and thankful when I finally gave her the fruit snacks. I think this is starting to work!

**Tami:** Back in the corner for the fifth time: We went a couple of hours from the last incident to now, with peace and quiet, which represents a big improvement. But then, while playing with her sister, the screaming erupted. So here we go again. I really hope this works.

**Elizabeth:** Just a caution here: At this point, if you start using this technique for everything, its effectiveness will quickly wear off. Right now, you should ONLY use it for whining and crying. Give her the impression that this habit is particularly unacceptable and that's why she gets this particularly tough treatment.

**Fawna**: Okay ladies! I've been following this exchange and I tried it last night with my Barry who just turned two last month. Failing to get his way last night with his big brother, he immediately commenced to wail. So I looked at him and said, "Oh, if you're going to cry, you must do it in the corner, Honey." I said this with a smile, then set him in the corner. When he tried to get up, all I had to say was, "Stay there, Barry!" He actually turned back around and resigned himself to staying there! I was amazed!

I thought for sure I would have to fight him on that one! He cried for about five minutes—pathetic, woe-is-me crying, while I played with his siblings. Every time he would turn to look at us I would say, "No Baby, sit there and finish crying." After a period of silence I said, "Oh, are you done?" He tentatively started to scoot towards me to test my reaction. I held out my arms and he climbed into my lap. I told him, "It's much better when you're not whining and crying, isn't it?"

This morning, when he started in again as usual, I said, "Oh, do you need the corner again?" and he immediately stopped! I was shocked! I didn't let him see my surprise, but I could have picked my chin up off the floor! Thank you, thank you, Elizabeth!

**Elizabeth:** Sounds like your little fellow is a quick learner, Fawna. Now just continue to be consistent with this. Crying equals The Corner.

**Tami:** I haven't had to repeat the corner treatment since the fifth time last night. She did start to fuss a bit and I said, "If you're going to fuss, do you know where you can do that?" She said, "In the corner." The tears stopped and I haven't heard a peep from her. Ordinarily, she would have already had a fit or two by this time of day. Thanks for this excellent solution!

**Tami** (two days later): Just an update. Yesterday, we didn't have to do the corner at all! She was corrected with a swat a couple times for disobedience, but quickly dried it up when I told her to. At one point she started to fuss at her sister and was about to go into a screaming fit. All I said was, "Do you want to cry in the corner?" She said, "No Mama," and the crying was over. Thanks a million!

*A scoffer does not love one who reproves him, he will not go to the wise.*

*- Proverbs 15:12*

## Learning the Hard Way

**Grace:** Okay, here's the short version. Ever since our latest baby was born seven months ago, our kids have spiraled downhill in both their behavior and attitudes. Of course, we've always had an excuse: we're all adjusting to the new baby, the kids are tired, Mom's tired, somebody's sick. Then, Mom fell sick for a week and dad took over and let them run wild.

Finally, my husband and I confronted the excuses, and the truth is we've become incredibly inconsistent. We have been tolerating impudent back talk, and we have responded in anger far too often.

So, in an effort to remedy matters, I conducted a family forum this morning on the kids' need to be obedient and to honor their parents. I told them that Mom and Dad have a job too: to love them, and to train them with discipline—not punish out of anger. At the end of my short lecture, I laid down the law: no more bickering, whining, and back-talking. Violators would be sent to the corner immediately every time.

Within five minutes, both boys were sent to the corner. I followed your cure for "The Screamer." Ruddy, after twenty minutes of sitting, said, "Sorry," and has been playing nicely all day since. Joel, however, is testing me. He has been in the corner much of the day.

Here's the problem. He will not obey in the corner. He keeps turning around and talking to his siblings. He grabs at them if they walk past him, and he keeps pestering me to release him. His attitude is nasty.

What do I do? I know that he fully expects me to get angry, yell at him, and then spank. I am determined not to lose my temper like that, but it's a real trial! For example, a few minutes ago he asked for a blanket to sit on because the tiles are cold. Then, instead of sitting on it, he kept dropping it on his head and playing. I took the blanket away and now he wants a book. I keep stopping every sentence with, "Joel, be quiet and face the wall. Every time you speak you are adding time to how long you are going to be there." It doesn't seem to be helping.

Do I spank him, or what?

**Elizabeth**: By all means, spank him. Some children will only learn the hard way. He is deliberately defying you, and doesn't plan to quit until you yield. So the next time he speaks or turns around, spank. If necessary, post yourself next to him with paddle in hand. Don't speak or argue with him. If he wants to make this into a battle, oblige him with the paddle.

Don't tell him you are adding on more time. That just sounds like a threat. Do tell him that he stays until you are convinced he is ready to obey.

Don't make him comfortable! What's with the blanket!? Make him a little UNcomfortable. If he persists, make him more uncomfortable. Make him stand up and put his hands on his head and give him a swat if he puts them down. (Use common sense—every once in a while have him put them down or shake them so they get some circulation—but then make him put them right back up there again.) Don't explain why you are doing this; he will soon realize that the way to get comfortable again is to give in and obey.

**Grace:** I finally won at 3:30 p.m. and he has been a joy ever since!

I hovered over him and delivered a swat each time he peeped. I also made him stand facing the corner with his arms straight up in the air while he counted to fifty. If he put his arms down, I made him start over. THREE times, he reached forty-nine and put his arms down. I made him start over each time.

I can't imagine why he would punish himself this way, but he did. After he finally counted to fifty with his arms raised, I let him put his arms down, but still made him stand in the corner another ten minutes. He apologized and has been a new child ever since.

In conclusion, let me say this is the first time in the past four months that I didn't lose my temper and let him win. No doubt he will test me again, probably to see if he can win with Dad. We are both determined to win though, and break this cycle of hysteria! Thanks!

**Elizabeth:** Wonderful work, Grace! Now save this and tape it to your refrigerator as a reminder for next time.

*Whoever loves discipline loves knowledge, but he who hates reproof is stupid.*

*- Proverbs 12:1*

## Untamed Whining Leads to Misery

*Dear Elizabeth,*

*I never allowed my children to whine and I make no exception for my grandchildren. I simply found it unbearable. Now I see a far better reason than my personal irritation to disallow such behavior.*

*The best reason is that a whining, pouting, tantruming child is truly miserable, a fact that sunk in recently when I spent a day with a friend and her two-year-old grandson. What an experience! That child whined for*

***everything…first time…every time****. "Just-on-the-verge-of-tears" whining was his habitual day-long demeanor. He was truly miserable.*

*So now I correct more for the sake of the children's own happiness than because I find them irritating. Now, if I swat a grandchild's bottom for pouting after a reprimand, and say, "No pouting. Play and have a good time," I am doing it to render the child's life joyful. I am setting up this child for future success and happiness by consistently helping him to reject and transcend the frustrations and anger that will poison his future paths.*

*Correcting behavior does not drive a child to bury or deny his feelings. Rather, he learns he has a choice regarding those things he will think and act on. One cannot think good thoughts and smile while stewing and sulking in anger. Try it.*

*Another major reason I discipline pouting is because every minute of pouting, whining, and rebellion is a minute outside of God's desire for us, and of happiness lost. In correcting my grandchildren for this, I am teaching them to do as we are told in Philippians 4:8-9: "Finally, brethren, whatsoever things are true, whatsoever things are honest, whatsoever things are just, whatsoever things are pure, whatsoever things are lovely, whatsoever things are of good report; if there be any virtue, and if there be any praise, think on these things." I am teaching my grandchildren to dwell on, think about, and ponder what is good, knowing that their reward will be genuine, radiant joy.*

*Yours truly,*
*Sandra, mother of five, grandmother of ten*

*For to a person who is good in His sight He has given wisdom and knowledge and joy….*

*- Ecclesiastes 2:26*

# eleven

# TEMPER TANTRUMS

*An angry man stirs up strife, and a hot-tempered man abounds in transgression.*
*- Proverbs 29:22*

## Are Temper Tantrums Acceptable?

Some parents, particularly those who have imbibed from the fountains of modern psychology, believe that temper tantrums are acceptable. They believe that it is necessary and good for a child to vent his frustrations, release tension, and express himself without restraint. They go so far as to believe it is the child's right to do so. I vigorously disagree.

Children seldom truly outgrow such willful expressions. The toddler tantrums are merely replaced by adult tantrums such as swearing, yelling, road rage, abusing animals, spousal or child abuse. Sometimes, they escalate to vicious assaults and murder. I don't see how anyone could dare defend the behavior that leads to such evils, yet the "experts" do it every day, and are extolled for it in the bargain. The advice to ignore tantrums abounds in the psychology books. Throw them out.

I see only evil in the uncurbed display of rage, selfishness, and willfulness. Because it is my responsibility to do my best to shape my children's character into what conforms to the image of God, I must never cease working to help them become loving, self-disciplined, godly human beings. I am obligated to step in and curb temper tantrums and any other kind of wrong behavior. This is why I was given the gift of children. This is why I am a mother.

> *Like a city that is broken into and without walls is a man who has no control over his spirit.*
>
> *- Proverbs 25:28*

## The "Frustration" Excuse

**Faith:** My fourteen-month-old has temper tantrums that usually seem to stem from frustration. Normally, they occur when he has difficulty getting a toy to work, or when his efforts to do something are frustrated. How much can I expect of my fourteen-month-old? Can I really expect him not to become frustrated?

**Elizabeth:** My experience with young children has caused me to conclude that very few truly throw fits because they are "frustrated." Perhaps frustration plays into the equation somewhere, but when the fit-throwing begins, the emotion these children are experiencing and displaying is *anger,* not frustration. A frustrated child will cry pitifully in helplessness and sadness. An angry child, hoping to force his will upon the situation, will allow his temper to flare out of control and throw an angry fit of rage instead. That's why they are called TEMPER tantrums—because they involve TEMPER.

Perhaps an incident begins with the child trying, and failing, to put a square block in a round hole. Perhaps he tries a few times and then begins to react. A truly frustrated child will sob in self-pity or run weeping to Mom for comfort. An angry child will throw a fit, hoping to force that block to fit in that hole, inflicting his own frustration on everyone. This is NOT frustration, but selfish anger. It may have started as frustration, but it quickly and wrongly turned to anger.

I do not allow temper tantrums in my home and so even if my children are frustrated, they do not have them. I teach them to ask me for help if they need it, and never to get angry and throw a fit just because they can't do something. A fourteen-month-old child is certainly capable of learning this. In fact, it is about the *best* age for teaching this. At this age, they are old enough to understand and obey, and the bad habit of indulging their temper can be easily checked at this age.

The longer you pacify a child in this area, by comforting, ignoring, or distracting, the worse the situation will become. The longer you let it go on, the harder it will be to stop the increasing tantrums you will be forced to endure. A tantrum that begins as frustration may not be rebellion against the parent at first, but it will soon become so. Before long, he will realize that he can throw a fit when he is challenged with the word "no" from his parents, or when he can't get his way in some matter or choice. If he obtained sympathy and understanding with his "frustration" fits, he will expect the same response to his "selfish" fits. Never allow frustration to be an excuse for a temper tantrum.

*Cease from anger, and forsake wrath; do not fret, it leads only to evildoing.*

*- Psalm 37:8*

## Ignoring the Tantrum

**Marie:** I always ignore my child when he throws a tantrum because ignoring the behavior teaches that it will gain no attention. Don't you agree with this?

**Elizabeth:** I agree, that *if* the child's purpose is to get attention, and you ignore him, he won't be rewarded with the attention he wants, and might eventually stop demanding it in this manner. I'm rather concerned about what he'll start doing as an alternative strategy.

In reality, few toddlers throw tantrums just to get attention. That's more easily and efficiently obtained in other ways. What motivates and fuels most tantrums is this: the child isn't getting his arbitrary demands gratified, and he is angry about it. The tantrum is simply a display of unrestrained anger. It's that elemental. Yes, he wants you to witness his anger, but that's secondary.

> *When the scoffer is punished, the naive becomes wise; but when the wise is instructed, he receives knowledge.*
> *- Proverbs 21:11*

## My Experience

My first two children indulged in a tantrum or two when they were small, but I managed to stop them somehow. I'm not sure how I did it; I just did, probably by becoming angry and shouting at them—never an acceptable option. Fortunately, they did it infrequently, and quit before the age of three. This was previous to the time I changed my parenting methods.

Other parents aren't so fortunate. I had a neighbor whose five-year-old regularly exploded in tantrums that amazed me. The mother's solution was to simply walk away and ignore him. Why she would do that, and why she would believe it a solution—when it obviously showed no sign of working even after five long years—I have no idea. But I was never tempted to follow her example.

When my third child reached two, he began throwing tantrums I couldn't stop. None of the childrearing books I'd read had any advice that helped. I really could not ignore him, so one day I handed him off to his father. Dad was equally helpless. He actually blamed me, demanding that I *"do something!"* That got me mad. I took my child and picked him up and yelled at him to "STOP IT RIGHT NOW!" It took him a few seconds, but he did stop. Undoubtedly, my own anger convinced him I meant business. Still, I don't recommend that method. Yelling is never an acceptable solution.

My husband and I realized that we would need to adopt a whole new parenting methodology to manage tantrums. The next time our child dropped to the floor in enraged screaming, I stood him up instantly and delivered a serious swat on the rear, saying "Stop it." I did not yell this time. I may have had to repeat my command, and I certainly had a stern "don't mess with me" demeanor, but never again did I yell. Surprised by the ambush and the swat, he pulled himself together rapidly. This made me realize that a tantruming child is not as out of control as they'd like us all to believe, and that the solution to tantrums is in the timing and the parent's bearing, not the yelling.

I've had seven additional children and none indulged in temper tantrums. To be sure, most of them tried it a time or two, but the *swift, certain, ambush* approach worked with them all.

> *He who is slow to anger is better than the mighty, and he who rules his spirit, than he who captures a city.*
>
> *- Proverbs 16:32*

## Catch It Early

The essential keys to success in tantrum stopping are **timing** (catching it *before* it becomes a full-blown tantrum), and **consistency** (catching and stopping *all* tantrums promptly, *every* time).

My later children never entered the full-blown temper tantrum stage, and here's an example demonstrating why. I remember one of my later children—he was one and a half years old—entering the kitchen crying for a toy. Since it was nothing urgent and I was occupied, I responded with, "Just a minute." He understood, but intensified the crying to dramatize his displeasure and demanded I do something about it *immediately*.

He looked at me with an *"I'm telling you what I want right now and you're not going to tell me to wait"* kind of look. To underscore his pique, he dropped abruptly to his rear and began to crank up the volume. He was swearing at me in toddler language.

I was not about to ignore him. Instead, I chose to nip it in the bud. I took him by the arm, demanding, "Get up," as I raised him to his feet. Then I said, "Stop it. Be quiet," and paused for him to comply. Leading him firmly across the kitchen, I placed him where I could watch and control him better and told him firmly to "wait." Before he could get too bored and let his mind wander back to the tantrum idea, I gave him a direction—"Get your book and bring it here." I wanted to test him to see if he was still inwardly rebellious or not, and I also wanted to focus his mind more on obeying than protesting. I gave him the toy he wanted only after he was completely composed and acting suitably.

Because he stopped crying immediately, I did not spank him, or scold him, or anything else. The reason he stopped immediately was because I addressed the issue *promptly*, and because I had been *consistently* teaching him for the previous six months to obey me in everything I asked. Since he was in the habit of obeying, he complied when I told him to do something. He had respect for my authority and he knew I meant what I said.

The best way, and sometimes the only way, to stop tantrums is to catch and correct the child when that ugly, pouting look first appears, *prior* to a full-fledged tantrum. If you are watching your child, you can easily detect heart signs. Read them accurately, and ambush the child with an *immediate* correction.

*A rebuke goes deeper into one who has understanding than a hundred blows into a fool.*

*- Proverbs 17:10*

## The "Post-Spanking" Tantrum

**Lydia:** The only time my daughter throws a temper tantrum is immediately after a spanking. One swat for some disobedience sets her off into crying, kicking, screaming, and stomping. Should I just say, "Stop," and then spank again if she doesn't stop? How can I expect her to stop when I just spanked her?

**Elizabeth:** Since you've only given her one swat, it doesn't sound to me as though she is throwing this type of fit because of the actual discomfort of the spanking. Nope, she's just mad. Mad that you dared to say "no" to her and insist she obey you. She is angry, not in pain. So address her attitude.

If you just spanked her, you should be next to her, so be ready and prevent her from throwing herself on the floor. Make her stay standing up. Minimize struggling with her, but do prevent her from getting her way or from hurting herself or you. Apply another swat and order her to stand up if she is resisting. Pause. Repeat. Remain calm and determined. Take your time. Outlast her.

It will help to speed things up if you keep her in some physical position that conveys your resolve to resist her, and also makes continued defiance increasingly uncomfortable. For example, a little boy I know pulled this on his mom the other day in my presence. It began when his mom told him "no." His knees buckled and he started to drop to the floor screaming. His mom and I were right there and we caught him by the arms and would not allow him to make it all the way down to the floor. We told him to stand up, but he refused. He pulled his knees up to his chest and held his feet up off the ground. Well, we just held him there in the uncomfortable suspended-in-mid-air position he had chosen and kept telling him to stand. He kept screaming, but it wasn't too long before he became too tired to hold his feet up off the ground any longer. The discomfort motivated him to give in, place his feet on the ground, and stand up.

That wasn't the end of the tantrum, but it was the beginning of the end. We persevered, not allowing him to do anything he wanted, and made him choose to do what we wanted instead. We did give him a swat on the bottom now and then to remind him that we were not giving in, and eventually he consented to obey us and stop the screaming, twisting, and kicking. The whole ordeal took perhaps ten minutes. After he calmed down, we made him stand facing the corner for about ten minutes or so. Next, we tested him with a few commands, then let him go, following up with rigorous Tomato Staking.

Try this with your daughter every time she throws a fit. Be ready for her when you have to spank her, knowing that she is likely to protest your correction with a temper tantrum. Catch her instantly; correct her firmly. Safely restrain her if needed, not allowing her to injure herself or others. If a struggle ensues, it often helps to command the child to do something specific that you can enforce. If she indicates that *she* wants to do one thing, insist she do the opposite. Do not give in to anything, however minor—she is trying to distract you and get around you.

Remember that you have all day. Remember that your purpose as a mother is to train her in godliness. Be determined and confident. Not rushed, or timid, or worried that it won't work. OUTLAST her.

> *An angry man stirs up strife, and a hot-tempered man abounds in transgression.*
>
> *- Proverbs 29:22*

## Tiptoeing Around Tantrums

**Donna:** My two-year-old son has always been soooo strong willed. I am *very* consistent, as is my husband, and although we made some mistakes when he was younger due to inexperience, we have been really on track since he was a year old. Although he is usually pretty good, I still dread almost every day because of his temper. When he doesn't get his way, he screams and kicks. It's a constant battle. Even though I always outlast, I always make him change his attitude (not just the behavior), and I always win. When we are finished, he is contrite and happily complies with my initial request. These battles last anywhere from five minutes to forty-five minutes, but I persist and stay calm. This can happen five times a day on a bad day. I am so tired of it! I dread seeing "The Look" that comes across his face just before he blows up. What am I doing wrong?

**Elizabeth:** Hmmm. It sounds like you are doing everything right, but since he is continuing to throw fits, there must be something we are missing here. One question I have is whether or not you give him direct, regular commands throughout the day. Does he usually respond well to direct commands? Or does he frequently resist them?

If he has a tendency to resist direct commands, I would really push that issue with him. I'd give him plenty, and be prepared for a possible battle each time. I'd meet any resistance by pushing him into the confrontation he is asking for, being certain I won. I'd do this as often as he resists any request.

Never cajole him into obeying. Could that be what is happening? Obviously, he is still not convinced that you are his rightful authority. He still feels he can control you, at least some of the time. The temper tantrums are his way of letting you know that he is in charge. When it strikes his fancy, he blows up with a tantrum, and although you eventually subdue him, he still nurtures the hope and expectation of ruling over you the next time around.

**Donna:** In general, he is well behaved. The tantrums only happen when I give him a direct command that's against his wishes. But you know, there are times when we do cajole him into obeying for fear of that out-and-out battle we know might come if we cross him. When the battle is evident, I NEVER let him win, but I wonder if I avoid a battle before it starts sometimes. Thanks so much for your help—you are a blessing to me! I will definitely make the command thing an issue and attempt to give him orders when he is entering the "anger zone" tomorrow.

**Elizabeth:** I think many parents of young children prone to tantrums soon begin dreading the upcoming confrontations so much that they start tiptoeing around their children. They begin using counting, distraction, appeasement, or similar devices, any time a touchy subject comes up. They hope and pray things won't turn into a tantrum.

That's a big mistake. It is far better to use your authority when your child first begins to think about resisting you—*before* he has decided to explode. Watch for that little hesitation. Watch for that little show of resistance. Watch for "The Look," as you called it, that indicates he is thinking about rebelling. Challenge any of these and other little signs *then,* when he is still a bit uncertain. Bring the rebellion out into the open with a direct command and correct it by insisting he obey you.

If close supervision and correcting for the little things pushes a child into a confrontation with you, it is a clear sign that he *needed* a good confrontation to clear up the issue of who is in charge. Go on and have that confrontation and *win.* If you do it well, and do it every time, only a few days should pass before you see a big change in his attitude of respect for you, and consequently how well he obeys and behaves in general.

**Donna:** It's been several days and I wanted to update you and give encouragement to others experiencing the same thing. Although I have been called the "Queen of Consistency" by family members, I now realize that I often give my son a couple chances to obey me, just to avoid an escalation to the tantrum level. I have been avoiding confrontation—not all the time—but I have been inconsistent with making him obey me the first time, every time. This is hard to admit, but this has been my fault. I feel horrible for allowing this rebellious spirit to grow in him. I didn't realize I was doing this, but I am so glad I realize it now.

So after thinking about this, I have been doing ultra-retraining with him and things are going much better. In the past, he was having tantrums five or six times a day that lasted from thirty to forty minutes each. Now, over the past three days, he has had only two, and they've lasted under ten minutes each time. He is so pleasant most of the time now, and he seems to be able to stop his tantrums before they really start. Thank you for your advice and encouragement! This godly instruction has surely saved my son and our whole family from much future pain, and is giving us joy in the meantime with a much happier two-year-old. I am staying on top of him. It is still early, but I am seeing results already.

**Followup from Donna:** It's been a year and I'm thrilled at what a sweet three-year-old my little boy is now! He is a changed little man! Praise the Lord! It is amazing how consistent discipline can truly change the heart of a child! He smiles and obeys happily and respectfully. He is a wonderful example of an obedient child (and his mommy is a beautiful example of a godly mother training her children for the Lord!). Come on everyone! Raise those standards and expectations for your children. Tantrums and bad tempers are not acceptable. You CAN do this!

*Do not associate with a man given to anger; or go with a hot-tempered man, lest you learn his ways, and find a snare for yourself.*

*- Proverbs 22:24-25*

# Part IV

# With Character In Mind

*Thanks Elizabeth for your website. I have witnessed firsthand how well-trained, obedient children can be such a JOY and HELP even during difficult times. Who says that little children are a burden? Mine have been such an asset to me!*

**Tamara**

# twelve

# PRIDE PROBLEMS

*These are the proverbs of King Solomon of Israel, David's son. He wrote them to teach his people how to live – how to act in every circumstance, for he wanted them to be understanding, just and fair in everything they did.*
*- Proverbs 1:1-3 (TLB)*

## Our Purpose: A Godly Child

Once proper respect for parents has been achieved and your authority recognized, a constant undercurrent of rebellion should no longer exist in your home. There should no longer be constant power struggles or recurring temper tantrums. Peace and joy should reign in general. When your child does transgress, a few words of rebuke should suffice to straighten out the matter. Of course, our parenting career is not over just because we've made it through the most difficult stage—that of gaining our child's respect. But now our job should at least be manageable. Now that the worst is over, we can slow down and view parenting more with an eye toward shaping the character of our child—just as that old tomato stake shapes and supports the tomato plant until it is strong, mature, and fruitful.

In the next few chapters, I am going to share a number things I've learned over the years with regard to different aspects of character training and nurturing in children. Dispersed between my ponderings are many more questions from parents regarding ongoing problems they are having with their children. I hope that my practical suggestions to these parents will help illustrate the principles I am trying to convey.

I have labeled and arranged these stories according to the character issue I felt was most pronounced in each case—not only to make them easier to locate and refer back to, but also in order to draw attention to your real purpose in disciplining:

***We should not be disciplining and training just to produce a mannerly child we can show off in public, but in order to bring our beloved children into conformity to the image of Christ, so that they will be well prepared in their hearts and habits when God calls them into His service.***

As you read on, please notice that it's not all about spanking, or even about keeping your child at your side, tightly Tomato Staked, 24/7. That part should be should be over with, and you should be moving on to a *lifestyle* of looser Tomato Staking, involving much teaching, mentoring, nurturing, and fellowshipping, punctuated with occasional discipline, adjusted to the individuality of each child and situation.

Most of the following pages will still refer to toddlers through the grade school ages. Older children and teens will be mentioned briefly later on and perhaps in a later book.

*It is by his deeds that a lad distinguishes himself if his conduct is pure and right.*

*- Proverbs 20:11*

## Arrogance

As I first began organizing this material by character quality, I noticed that arrogance and pride started popping up in a great number of the stories and letters. It became obvious to me that pride is at the root of many, many of the behavioral issues we have with our children. So I decided to gather some of the most obviously pride-related problems together and cover them all in one chapter. So here we are.

Rather than focusing immediately on correcting the child's symptoms of arrogance in this first go-round, I'd like to indict the parents of the typically arrogant child, for they are the ones largely at fault. Sure, all children have a tendency toward pride and arrogance. We are all born self-centered, and from there it is a very short step to selfishness, then pride. Most adults still have unresolved pride issues, and if they don't see or won't admit to the vice in themselves, they will certainly not see it in their precious children. Excuses ensue and disaster awaits.

When their child is small and *demands* to put on his own shoes without their help, they will overlook his attitude and believe he is just demonstrating the first signs of self-reliance and eagerly accommodate him. When he gets a little older and *insists* on choosing which clothes he wears every morning, they will overlook his spirit again. They think he is just naturally blessed with good color-sense and will encourage him with even more freedom of choice.

When he begins *commanding* other children in regard to the best way to play every game, and *correcting* them regarding every topic they bring up to discuss, his parents will once more miss the state of his heart. They will simply see their child as smarter than the rest of the children in the world and congratulate themselves on what a good job they did birthing and educating him. And so it goes, until one day they wake up and find they have a ten-year-old (or younger) telling *them, and other adults,* what to do. Suddenly, he's pointing out to them the error of their ways, confidently believing that he is better and smarter than they (and therefore has the right to do so!).

To get us started with the problem of arrogance, here's a short letter illustrating the symptoms of pride overlooked in a child, and the parental excuses given instead:

**Audrey:** My six-year-old does something that disturbs me, but I'm not sure what to do about it. He has a habit of trying to joke with adults as if he is on their level. For example, when I go to the doctor and I joke around with her, he feels he can join in too, even though I have explained to him that she is an adult, and a doctor, and should be treated with respect.

I think it's hard for him because as a family we like to laugh and joke around. He just doesn't know when to stop, and he also seems not to see himself on a different level from the adults. Any suggestions on how to stop this behavior and provide appropriate outlets for his need to entertain?

**Elizabeth**: When a child is above the toddler age and doesn't seem to be catching on to your verbal teaching, and does this sort of thing repeatedly, it's time to examine yourself to see if perhaps you are contributing by allowing him to become pridefully puffed up within your home.

How do you allow your child to talk to *you*? Do you give him the impression that his opinions are just as valuable as yours? Do you let him think he is just as wise as you? That he has the right to interrupt and speak his mind at any time at home? If you are allowing him to think he is on equal footing with the adults at home, he will logically believe the same applies outside the home, and will act accordingly.

The first thing you need to do to correct this is to stop making excuses for him. He is not doing it because you joke around at home, or because he "has a need to entertain." He is doing it because he erroneously, and with pride, believes he is your equal and therefore has the same rights as all other adults, particularly in the area of speaking his mind. You need to determine how you are encouraging this mindset at home and you need to take serious steps to reverse the trend.

*Do not be wise in your own eyes; fear the LORD and turn away from evil.*

*- Proverbs 3:7*

## Sulking

Here's another example of a parent not recognizing a problem as one of pride, and hence not addressing it properly:

**Lindsey:** My six-year-old has a problem with talking to me about matters that bother her. When upset, instead of coming to me, she'll go sit by herself, often to pout or cry. When I approach her, she will sit with me, but won't tell me what's wrong. I can ask her, "Did you hurt yourself? Did Mommy do something that upset you? Did your sister do something to you?" But she'll only shake her head and sadly say, "No." When I ask her what *did* happen, she'll either say she doesn't want to talk about it or she will just remain silent. Eventually, she gets over it.

When this behavior occurs, what should I do? Should I persist in trying to find out what is wrong? Should I keep trying to convince her to discuss it with me, or should I just let it go?

**Elizabeth:** I strongly suspect that you are feeling sorry for her and perhaps feeling a little guilty yourself, thinking you might be the cause of her misery. Don't be deceived. This sounds like self-pity and manipulation to me, which are simply derivatives of pride. I would ask her what she was pouting about and I would expect an answer. I would not accept her refusal to respond. If I really thought she wanted to tell me, but was being held back by shyness, then I might do some gentle probing, but even then, I would ultimately expect an honest answer.

What I sometimes do in similar situations, when a child refuses to answer me, is to have him sit quietly at the table for a while. Then I ask him again. If he is still resistant, I let him know that he won't be leaving the table until he is ready to have an honest discussion with me. I don't get angry with him, but I don't back down either. Yes, I outlast him. He *must* learn to set aside his pride and communicate.

This is one of the most important things you can ever teach your child. It is unacceptable for a person to clam up and punish everyone with his silence. He may appear to be heartbroken over some injustice, but it's really just a slight injury to his pride that he has turned into manipulation and vindictiveness. The longer a child holds out and gives you The Silent Treatment, the more it indicates that he arrogantly believes he has the right to act this way. I wouldn't want to deal with such a person as an adult, and I can't even imagine being married to someone like this. As always, your job is to teach godliness. Learning not to manipulate, but to humbly communicate, is an important part of godliness.

*"Come now, and let us reason together," says the LORD...*
*- Isaiah 1:18*

## Disrespect

**Esmeralda:** How do you handle back-talk? I am not talking about outright rebellious sassing; I mean when children pout in response to a request or habitually ask that requests be deferred. Sometimes I have observed these responses tainted by a mean look or verbal anger. Are these times that you would spank? I'm reluctant to spank because these children are expressing how they feel in the only way they know how. Please give me some guidance.

**Elizabeth:** They are "expressing how they feel in the only way they know how"? Oh dear, red psychobabble flags are going up all over. Never mind.

Okay, stop immediately. Instead of excusing your child, correct him and educate him. If this is the only way he knows to express his feelings, you need to teach him a more acceptable alternative NOW.

This is not too hard with young children. Teach them and then *require* them to look you in the eye and politely say, "Yes, Mom," when you ask them to do something. Do not allow the stamping of feet, or whining, or other similar hints of a disgruntled spirit. You can discourage those symptoms in different ways. One is to tell them, "Now go back and do that again with a smile this time," or something similar. Repeat until they display a good attitude. Remember that with a young child, if you can change the outside, the inside will invariably follow suit.

It is unacceptable for a child to pout when given a parental command. Forget the modern drivel that says a child must "express his feelings." If his "feelings" are wrong, he needs to learn how to change them and show appropriate respect for the mother God placed in authority over him. He needs to learn to set aside his own desires and obey the commandment that says: *"Honor your father and your mother."* The Bible contains no loophole permitting disrespect to one's parents just because a child is "expressing his feelings."

> *"Honor your father and your mother, as the Lord your God has commanded you, that your days may be prolonged, and that it may go well with you on the land which the Lord your God gives you."*
>
> *- Deuteronomy 5:16*

## Bossiness

**Lena:** My firstborn, a son, is almost four. Since turning three, he has been challenging us much more, which I think is normal. He seems better than a few months ago, praise the Lord, but he still will occasionally point his little toddler finger at my husband or me and say something like, "No, Mommy, that's MY job," or "No, Daddy, that's NOT how you do it."

Sometimes it seems harmless, while at other times there seems to be a serious underlying negative attitude to go with it. Please help us. We need some wisdom and I'm praying the Lord might use you to illuminate the issue for us.

**Elizabeth:** It is common for parents think they should overlook everything that is "normal." I disagree. I don't believe that just because something is "normal" means it is right. As a Christian, I believe that we all are born with a tendency to do the wrong thing at times. So it is "normal" for a child to do the wrong thing at times.

That's why God gave children parents. We parents have the job of stopping the "normal" bad things a child does, and replacing them with good habits. Any time your child displays attitudes and behaviors that are wrong, and bossiness is certainly wrong, then you can and should correct them. You are right to seek out a solution.

Begin by telling him that what he is doing is wrong and he must not do it. With a two or three-year-old, you might say, "Don't tell Daddy what to do. Ask Daddy what *he* wants *you* to do." Then make him do as you say. In an older child, you might say, "You sound very bossy, proud, and disrespectful. Don't talk that way to your father. If you want to make a suggestion, word it like this...."

In all instances, stop the bossiness quickly, then instruct the child on what he should be doing, saying, and thinking. See that he demonstrates to you the correct way to act so you know he understands and also so that you know he has a spirit willing to humbly take instruction.

*And calling them to Himself, Jesus said to them, "You know that those who are recognized as rulers of the Gentiles*

> *lord it over them; and their great men exercise authority over them. But it is not so among you, but whoever wishes to become great among you shall be your servant; and whoever wishes to be first among you shall be slave of all. For even the Son of Man did not come to be served, but to serve, and to give His life a ransom for many."*
>
> *- Mark 10:42-45*

## Contrariness

**Mattie:** My five-year-old son is developing a habit I don't like, but I'm hard-pressured to give it a name. I tell him not to do "that," but I don't even know if he comprehends what I'm referring to. Here's what happens: Whatever the subject, he has to put in his two cents' worth and get in the last word. Quite often he goes beyond this to outright disagreement with whatever was said.

For example, if we're discussing plans for him to learn Spanish, he'll pop up with, "No, I want to learn Chinese." Or I'll say, "Take that toy off your head," and he'll say, "But I like it on my head." Recently, he heard me talking with a friend about the leaves falling early this year, and he interjected, "I don't see a single leaf." He's not obviously cocky or belligerent. Instead, he seems cheery and good-natured, but this behavior is progressing into a habit that goes beyond what I think is acceptable.

**Elizabeth:** Venturing from good-natured opinion into deliberate opposition is being "contrary," the first step toward becoming "argumentative." Again, this stems from arrogance on his part. He thinks his opinion should be valued as highly as yours and is intent upon proving it to you. So nip this in the bud to head off what will only degenerate. Whenever he exhibits his contrary mode, stop him and offer an appropriate model and insist he follow it. For example:

**Mom:** I really like it when the curtains are open and the sun shines in.

**Contrary child:** *(with a smile)* I like it better when it's dark in here.

**Mom:** Son, that is a foolish statement. Say: "I agree Mom, the sun is very nice shining in here."

**Child:** But Mom, I....

**Mom:** *(in a 'no joking' voice)* Say what I told you to say NOW and don't say anything else.

**Child:** I agree Mom, the sun is very nice shining in here.

**Mom:** That's better; now don't do that again.

Understand, that to precisely label this behavior for your child as being "contrary" is unnecessary. He has a conscience and knows he is transgressing, despite the absence of a precise label. He knows exactly what you mean when you order him to stop. At some point you will want him to know what being contrary is, how it reflects a rebellious proud heart, why no one likes it, and how damaging the habit can become. But for now, it's enough to just call it back-talking or arguing, and not allow it.

*Wise men store up knowledge, but with the mouth of the foolish, ruin is at hand.*

*- Proverbs 10:14*

## Haughtiness

**Belinda:** My eleven-year-old son displays a very self-centered, haughty attitude in our home. He is especially ugly to his eight-year-old sister and is becoming increasingly argumentative and disrespectful toward me too. It's been suggested that he needs to be "taken down a few pegs." While I agree I need to teach him humility, I'm concerned about how to do so without crushing his spirit. I know it will be painful for him, but I don't want to squash the child, just his haughty attitude. Any ideas?

**Elizabeth:** Belinda, if he is as you say, haughty, you are in no danger whatsoever of "crushing" or "squashing" him. In fact, you will probably find that it is very difficult to even make him feel genuinely embarrassed, let alone properly humbled and repentant. That's the way it is with a proud child, and that's why we must be prepared to double our efforts if we want to get these children to see that they are not "God's gift to the rest of mankind."

If we don't take up this challenge, they will eventually become haughty, arrogant adults no one can stand. Haughtiness, according to *Proverbs 6:16-19,* is one of the seven things *"the Lord hates"* and that are *"an abomination to Him."* This is a very serious matter, so please don't hesitate because you think you will hurt his feelings. You won't, and if you do, it will work toward your goal, not against it.

**Belinda:** But Elizabeth, he has a very sensitive side. It is so odd! He can be just as kind and empathetic as he is haughty! This is why I am feeling the need to be more careful than I might otherwise. When I talk more harshly to him than normal, he feels really bad about it. For example, yesterday, after a scolding, he asked me why I was "being so mean to him."

I recognize that what he feels bad about is how he is being treated, not about his wrongdoing. He continually turns things around to be about him. All he sees is himself as the one in the right, the victim. I can tell when he is truly repentant, and it is not as often as it should be. I am not sure how to get across how badly he is behaving in a way that he sees it, and yet not crush him.

**Elizabeth:** Please don't worry about crushing him. Proud people often appear sensitive, but it is only because their ego is easily bruised. Their pride makes them recoil from admitting they are ever wrong. They will argue, protest, manipulate, carry on, and do anything and everything they can think of to ensure that they do not look bad. They want to preserve their superior image.

What they really need, in order to acquire some humility, is a realistic picture of themselves—to be shown that they are not as great as they think they are. They need to have their ego bruised a bit. That's the whole idea behind being "taken down a few pegs."

**Belinda:** Okay, I think I understand. But when I do correct him, he wants to argue and protest and it doesn't seem to do any good. When I won't let him, he gets very angry. What do I do when he is haughty and ugly, or wants to argue? Do I continue to stop him? What do I say to him? I need some specifics, please!

**Elizabeth:** If he begins arguing with you, the first thing to do is cut him off and require him to remain silent. Have him sit near you for a while, doing and saying nothing. Then ask him if he is ready to listen respectfully to you and learn something. He'll probably say "yes," although he won't really mean it. He will only mean that he is willing to "act" respectful in terms of what he says, so he doesn't get into trouble from you.

That's not enough, but it's a start. You might then move to questioning him about his motives, attitudes, and actions in an attempt to prick his conscience. Persist, asking different thought-provoking questions, until you start getting him to really look at himself and what he is doing and thinking. Ask things like:

Do you really think that you know more than everyone else does?
Do you think you have always been right about everything?
Do you think that even if occasionally you *are* right, it's nice to brag about it?
What do you think it says about you when you pick on your sister?
Are you 100% in the right here or did you sin also?
Do you think you should be concerned about her sins or about your own sins?

As he responds, elaborate on the correct answer. Show him with black and white facts and concrete examples that he is not Mr. Wonderful. Go on like this until you see a glimmer of understanding in his eyes. A proud child is usually very reluctant to admit being at fault anywhere (but knows he is), and you have to keep whittling away at his ego with reason and evidence until he is forced to acknowledge his shortcomings.

Ask him if he understands how important humility is—elaborate. Point out Scripture to him. Then ask him how he thinks he is exemplifying humility. Tell him that a humble person is a person who can say "I was wrong." Ask your child if he can say that. Ask him if he can say that without adding: "But…." Require him to say he was wrong about whatever actions or attitudes precipitated this latest incident. Require him to sincerely apologize to the person he wronged if applicable.

When humbling a child, it is especially helpful to focus on honesty and gratitude. Ask him to honestly list his faults, and what in particular he did wrong in the latest incident, regardless of the other person's infraction. Show him that if he is honest, he will see that he is not the smartest, best-looking, most talented, etc., person on earth. Get him to see that even his good points are really only due to the care, teaching, love, attention, and resources of OTHERS, not himself.

In the end, in order for a proud child to be made humble, he must be able to honestly see his faults and be able to admit to them, and he must also see and be grateful to God and others for everything he has or is.

**Belinda at a later date:** Thank you for all the advice. It worked! My son is much better now, and rarely argues. Now he comes to us to say, "I was thinking that…. Do you think that is right?" How sweet it is when your son comes around and wants you to double-check him for errors before he speaks!

*If you have been foolish in exalting yourself or if you have plotted evil, put your hand on your mouth.*

*- Proverbs 30:32*

# Showing Off

**Maxine:** Frequently, my four-year-old asks me to observe as she strikes a dramatic pose designed to earn her praise. She seems to revel in admiration. This doesn't seem proper to me and I'm wondering if I'm encouraging this proud and vain behavior somehow. Is it possible I am praising her too much about the wrong things? What is causing this excessive self-focus?

**Elizabeth:** Yes, it is very possible that you are inflating her ego by flattering her in excess or by praising her about the wrong matters. That would account for her behavior. If a pure-hearted child brings me a picture he drew and wants me to look at it, I do, exclaiming over it and asking him questions about it. Soon the humble little artist is satisfied that Mom loves and approves of him, and he runs off to draw another picture.

However, if the same child draws an intentionally goofy picture, or stands on his head, or does some other conspicuously senseless thing, and cries, "LOOK AT ME!" or "LOOK AT WHAT I CAN DO!", my Mommy Radar goes off and I know I'm witnessing an egotistical episode of showing off. In that case I say seriously, "Okay, that's enough, you look ridiculous doing that. Go do something a mature child would do."

If you notice any inclination toward pride or vanity, limit praise to *only* praise for sincere acts of kindness and humility. Even then, don't gush over the child. Let him know you are pleased with him for these things, but only if he maintains a humble spirit for the duration.

> *Do nothing from selfishness or empty conceit, but with humility of mind let each of you regard one another as more important than himself.*
>
> \- *Philippians 2:3*

## Vanity

**Claudia:** I see disconcerting signs of vanity in my five-year-old. When shopping with me at age two and a half, she was able to match tops and bottoms together perfectly. I truly think she has a "beauty-loving heart," but perhaps because I've encouraged this, she is now also showing signs of an undue focus on her own appearance. These are the types of things she does very frequently:

- She puts her hair up in a variety of hairdos several times a day.
- She loves to play dress-up with old ballet outfits and does so at every opportunity.
- Whenever she can, she adorns herself with necklaces she makes out of beads.
- Every time she passes something reflective (mirror, window, TV), she pauses and savors looking at herself.

Admittedly, some of this is just common to childhood. I am not concerned about her desiring to be pretty, but I am anticipating the coming decades and wondering if I need to head-off what might swell into an alarming degree of vanity.

**Elizabeth:** I would institute some reasonable "limits." For example, tell her that she has to pick one hairdo for the day and leave it that way. I would not allow her to choose what clothes she wears every day. Allow that only occasionally. Don't let her play dress-up every day or change her clothes multiple times a day. Get rid of the mirrors too. (I removed full-length mirrors from my girls' room when they were small to prevent this type of thing. The mirrors reappeared when they were in their late teens and actually needed them.)

While you are doing all this, be sure to guide her into godly attitudes about appearance. Teach her with all diligence and sincerity that although God made many beautiful things, He loves inner beauty the most.

Ask her if she thinks that a pretty little girl who is sassing her mother still looks pretty. When you see another nicely dressed child misbehaving, point this out and say, "That little girl has a pretty dress, but you don't even notice it when she is acting so awful. The way she is acting makes her look ugly, don't you think?" When you see a lovely smile, point that out and say, "Wasn't that lady at the counter who helped us, beautiful? I didn't even notice her clothes, but she had such a friendly warm smile it just made her look beautiful." And so on. Teach, teach, teach. Instill values, then teach some more!

> *"But let him who boasts boast of this, that he understands and knows Me, that I am the LORD who exercises lovingkindness, justice, and righteousness on earth; for I delight in these things," declares the LORD.*
>
> *- Jeremiah 9:24*

## Precociousness

In the strictest definition of the word: "Wisdom beyond a child's years," precociousness actually sounds like a thing to be desired. However, the common usage of the word indicates the obnoxious "know-it-all" child that we all would prefer to avoid. Precociousness is only cute to naive or proud parents who are not looking toward the future consequences.

Have you been told you have a "precocious" child? If so, no matter how kindly or with what degree of humor it was said, it should not be taken as a compliment and it's time to examine your parenting for flaws that may be contributing to this very unattractive and damaging attribute.

Are you over-educating your child? Are you destroying his innocence and puffing him up by teaching him things that should be held back until he is older? Being a homeschooling parent myself, I know the joy of teaching and the temptation to want to teach everything possible. But a wise parent will restrain herself from teaching the wrong things, or things that should wait until the child becomes older and more mature.

A young child does not need to know all the medical "facts of life," for example. If an eight-year-old girl does not know all the graphic details of the birthing process, she won't be tempted to inappropriately join into an adult conversation and start advising an expectant mother on just how to "pant and blow."

If she has not been educated as to every minute detail of breastfeeding, she won't be tempted to instruct some new mother on the proper way the get her baby to "latch-on." Both of the aforementioned examples, if practiced, will surely earn your child an uncomely reputation as a "precocious" and perhaps even "obnoxious" child.

Even more important than what or how much you teach, is the *attitude* you convey as you teach, and the perspective you teach your child in regard to learning. Never give a child the impression that he knows all there is to know on any given subject. Be sure to repeatedly end your teaching sessions (whether formal or informal) by making the child aware that there is much more to learn about every subject, and whatever you just taught him is really only a drop in the bucket. Continually impress upon him that others, particularly adults, know far more than he does, and that he should feel honored when he has the opportunity to learn from others.

Be sure that your children do not believe that they even know more than other *children* do. Knowing *more* than others should not be their goal. There should be no *competition* between themselves and others to accumulate more facts and head knowledge. Their goal in acquiring knowledge should only be so that it might enable them to serve God and others better. And be sure that both you and they value wisdom of character far above head knowledge.

I recall, twenty-four years ago, proudly showing my father how my first-born son, then only two years old, could read. Instead of giving him (and me) a pat on the head and a "job well done," my dad soberly advised, "Just don't let him think he's too smart."

Humph. I was taken aback and admittedly even a bit miffed by this. But upon reflection, I recognized the wisdom in what my father had offered, and to this day I am very glad that I took it to heart. Do not let your children think they are too smart.

> *...we know that we all have knowledge. Knowledge makes arrogant.... If anyone supposes that he knows anything, he has not yet known as he ought to know.*
>
> \- *I Corinthians 8:1-2*

## Humility

Some believe that humility does not have to be taught in the home because the harsh realities of life outside the home will teach it well enough. But does "real life" always succeed in teaching humility? Obviously not. Many adults are monsters of pride—utterly devoid of humility and living lives that demonstrate it to all. Clearly, if humility is to be learned, it ought to be taught early, when your child is still in the home.

Instilling the virtue of humility in your child cannot be accomplished in one easy lesson. It requires constant, vigilant attention to be certain that this spirit permeates your whole household and your entire way of life.

Aside from the practical hands-on aids to teaching humility mentioned above, one of the most effective avenues toward this goal, is to teach our children awe and reverence for God's ways and works. It is difficult to consider the unimaginable grandeur and expanse of the universe without being struck by one's own insignificance. It is difficult to ponder the service of the saints throughout Scriptures and history without being brought low by our own lack of faith and modesty in comparison.

It is impossible to revere Christ, our great model for emulation, who throughout Scripture was presented as a humble servant, who, though King of Kings, disdained his rightful glory for the humble life of a man, washed the feet of his friends, and died a criminal's death for our redemption, without having our hearts pierced and our own unworthiness laid bare. What greater way to teach the preeminent virtue of humility, than to impress upon our children this picture and love, mercy, and truth?

*For through the grace given to me I say to every man among you not to think more highly of himself than he ought to think.*

*- Romans 12:3*

# thirteen

# SIBLING SQUABBLES

*But the fruit of the Spirit is love, joy, peace, patience, kindness, goodness, faithfulness, gentleness, self-control; against such things there is no law.*

*- Galatians 5:22-23*

## Sibling Problems

The cause of almost all the sibling problems I have encountered in my internet family can be boiled down to self-centeredness and pride. Since we've already discussed pride at some length, I'd like to move on to the natural selfishness of children, how it demonstrates itself in sibling problems, and what we can do about eradicating it and producing children who are peacemakers instead. Again, I will be using questions from parents to illustrate my points and perspectives and to deliver some practical help to those who are dealing with this issue in their families.

*Blessed are the peacemakers, for they will be called the sons of God.*

*-Matthew 5:9*

## Pre-Baby Jealousy

**Dacia:** My children are acting up more than usual lately. They know I am expecting a new baby. Are they jealous already? I want them to adjust well to their new sibling. What should I do?

**Elizabeth:** Please don't believe that when a new baby is introduced into the family the other siblings will automatically become jealous. This is simply not true and certainly not true in advance of the baby's arrival! Your children are not misbehaving because a new baby is coming. If there is any connection at all, it is very likely that they are misbehaving because you are treating them differently.

Are you distracted and not watching them as well as you normally do, thus allowing more temptations than usual? Is morning sickness making it difficult to spend as much time with them as they have grown accustomed to, enticing them to misbehave in order to get your attention? Is your concern about them adjusting to the new baby causing you to be more lenient with them, letting them get away with little things and thereby encouraging them to test the boundaries more and more? All these changes in behavior on your part are quickly noticed by your children and can cause them to alter their behavior—usually for the worse.

I never went to any great lengths to verbally lecture, educate, or "prepare" my children for the arrival of their next new sibling. Most little children aren't going to understand all the speeches anyway, and you can easily do more harm than good. Warning them about all the problems the new baby will create will just encourage them to expect such problems to occur.

For example: I never said things like, "It's hard having a new baby. You might be angry sometimes, so come to Mommy when you are upset and we'll talk about it." No, I thought it was far better to be pleasantly matter-of-fact about the upcoming event and just expect the whole family to take it in stride.

Whenever I was expecting a new little one, I just treated it as a normal, wonderful, *family* event. I referred to the babe as "our" new baby, not "Mom's" new baby, or "my" new baby, or even "the" new baby. I believed it is wonderful to have a new baby, so I acted as though the other children would feel the same way. And they always did.

Building up false hopes that the new baby will be "fun, fun, fun" all the time, can be just as damaging as dire warnings, so I didn't do that either. I didn't want them to be disappointed and resentful when the child arrived and they began to notice that crying, smelly diapers, and spit-up came with the package, and that Mom was suddenly very tired and preoccupied.

So I didn't overemphasize the entertainment value of the new child, but I did make sure they knew this wonderful event was a blessing from God and that the new arrival would be someone we would welcome and love. I told them they would be allowed to help care for the baby, and even hold him when he was a little bigger. I made it sound as though helping was a special treat, and that caring for and protecting the new baby was an important job they would soon have the privilege of experiencing.

Since I knew I would be more busy and distracted than normal once the baby was born, during pregnancy I tried to be even more diligent than usual to correct behavior problems in my other toddlers—to assure they would be under control when the new baby arrived and it became more difficult to handle such problems.

Besides correcting as needed for routine misbehavior, I also corrected any child who pouted or displayed other signs of a wrong attitude about the new arrival. I saw this as really no different than any other wrong attitude, and I dealt with it accordingly. I tried to handle things wisely, promptly, and properly, and the results were no significant sibling rivalry or jealousy.

*Take hold of instruction; do not let go. Guard her, for she is your life.*

*- Proverbs 4:13*

## Post-Baby Jealousy

**Allison:** My older daughter is almost three years old and we have been having a problem with her that seems to be related to her little sister. She won't stay in her bed during the night or at naptime. We are very consistent in correcting her each time she gets out, but she still keeps up the misbehavior. She wants to be in the baby's crib and the baby to be somewhere else.

**Elizabeth:** It sounds like your three-year-old may be a little jealous of her younger sibling. She is perhaps noticing all the consideration the baby in the crib is getting and feels a bit left out. Be sure to give her plenty of your attention whenever you see an opportunity.

Be very generous with hugs and cuddles and little chats together. Seek her out for these things, even if she does not come to you asking for them. Meanwhile, it is perfectly fine to treat them like twins for a while, until the older one feels more secure in your love and affection.

At our house, once the expected new baby was born, one of the things I did to discourage jealousy problems was making sure I was not always pushing the older children aside while I indulged and catered to the baby. Thus, if I was helping a toddler get a bowl of cereal, and the baby started to fuss, I did *not* drop everything, rush to pick up the baby, and leave my poor toddler staring at an empty bowl. I didn't want to leave him sitting there waiting and feeling neglected for the next half hour, while I comforted, nursed, burped, changed, and cuddled the baby. No, I calmly finished tending to the immediate needs of my toddler first, *then* I went and picked up the baby.

So be careful not to push the older one aside too soon. My best advice is to keep BOTH your children very close to you as much as possible, being lovingly demonstrative with them, but still not allowing manipulation or misbehavior. Stop all bickering and unkindness toward one another.

Try to encourage the older one to have a sense of responsibility toward the younger one, by having the older one help you with the younger. Meanwhile, teach the younger one to show love and appreciation to the older ones with hugs, kisses, and a cooperative spirit. As they grow, don't allow the older one to boss the younger around, but at the same time teach the younger one to respect the older one and obey polite requests.

> *Now for this very reason also, applying all diligence, in your faith supply…godliness, and in your godliness, brotherly kindness, and in your brotherly kindness, love.*
>
> *- II Peter 1:5-7*

## Sharing

Many childrearing "experts" say that children should not be required to share their toys. Some parents require them to share, but set timers to keep everything perfectly even. Some buy two of everything in an effort to ensure equality and stop the fighting over possessions. While these methods may temporarily relieve the stress of sibling toy wars, none of these methods appeal to me. None of them accomplishes the goal of training my children to have godly mindsets and godly habits.

As always, I use sharing as an opportunity to teach my children godly character. I look toward godly adult interaction for my teaching model. That means that I am not satisfied when my children are acting like self-centered, immature children, but I work toward the goal of having their behavior ultimately reflect the generosity, kindness, wisdom, and other character qualities found in a godly adult.

So, for example, if a child receives a toy for his birthday, I don't just declare the toy his and allow him to be as selfish with it as he pleases. Instead, I require him to act in the same way an adult gift recipient would act. Yes, the toy belongs to him and for a few days or weeks the other children are not to ask to share it. In the same way, if Mom just received a brand new sewing machine, her best friend would probably not rush right over and ask to borrow it, would she?

However, after the newness wore off, I would expect the birthday child to share his toy, if asked politely, and assured that the other child would care for it properly, just as Mom would lend out her sewing machine to a reliable friend if she asked.

There would be certain occasions where I would expect my child to politely refuse to share a particular item. Just as an adult would not normally lend out something that did not belong to him, for example, neither would I expect a child to do so. If the object in question was breakable or of special sentimental value, I would teach my child to ask my permission first before honoring another child's request to share it.

As is so often the case, you can't create and institute one simple edict that covers every situation. You have to be watching your children as they interact, guiding them, and making sure that they are all learning to share, or sometimes refuse to share, in a kind, godly way.

*"Give to him who asks of you, and do not turn away from him who wants to borrow from you."*

*- Matthew 5:42*

## Selfishness

**Claire:** Quarreling over toys is the one predictable daily event in our house. One child will have a toy, set it down, and wander off. A sibling opportunist comes along and claims it. The first child returns and cries, "Hey! That was mine!" And the fight is on! Although both are being selfish, still the original player is to blame, since he had abandoned the toy. Right?

To resolve the quarrels, I've resorted to a somewhat crude expedient: I set a timer for fifteen minutes. One plays with the toy in dispute until the timer beeps, then must hand it over to the other child for the next fifteen minutes. And so on and so forth.

I explain that they are learning to take turns and share, and this does make things tolerable when the timer is handy, but is there a better way to deal with the problem?

**Elizabeth:** While the timer may give you some temporary respite from sibling bickering, they are not learning to be generous and share out of the kindness of their hearts when they depend on a timer to rule them. Throw out the timer and loosely Tomato Stake them near you when they are playing, so you can observe their interactions. Step in and teach them not just how to follow egocentric rules (*I had it first so it's mine*), but godly principles (*it pleases God when I am generous and share, even if I had it first and it's mine*). Be there and demonstrate, supervise, teach, and enforce as needed.

Here is a model script to give you some ideas:

*(Johnny and Timmy engage in a tug of war over a toy car. Timmy is holding the car and Johnny is trying to pull it away.)*

**Mom:** Stop it right now!

*(neither lets go)*

**Timmy:** He's grabbing my car!

**Johnny:** It's my car!

**Mom:** Johnny, let go of that car.

*(Johnny reluctantly lets go, but looks dejected.)*

**Mom:** Johnny, if you want the car, ask him nicely for it. We do not grab. Say, "May I please have the car?" Go ahead and ask him now.

**Johnny:** *(to Timmy)* May I please have that car?

*(Timmy looks forlornly at mom.)*

**Mom:** Timmy, give him the car.

*(Timmy pouts and drops the car instead of putting it in his brother's outstretched hand.)*

**Mom:** Timmy, pick that up and hand it to your brother nicely.

*(Timmy needs a little swat to encourage him, but then obeys, still unhappy. Johnny prepares to escape with the car, but Mom stops him.)*

**Mom:** Johnny, who had the car first?

**Johnny:** *(hangs head)* He did.

**Mom:** Timmy, ask Johnny for the car back, nicely. Say, "May I please have my car back?"

**Timmy:** "May I please have my car back?"

*(By now Johnny knows what is up and hands the car back, though less than thrilled. After all, he didn't get what he wanted, but he recognizes that Mom is right.)*

**Mom:** *(to both)* Now I don't want to hear you fighting over that car again. Do *not* grab anything from anyone. If you want something, ask for it nicely. If your brother was just playing with something, don't grab it the second he sets it down. That is very selfish. Wait until you think he doesn't want it anymore, then ask him nicely for it. And do not claim a whole pile of toys just to keep them from your brother. That is hoarding, and it is very selfish and you will not be allowed to play at all if I see that happening. Do you understand?

*(Both children nod, and Mom allows them to play again, but keeps watch over them.)*

Now that's just an example. It needs to be adjusted according to the occasion and ages of the children. Keep it simple. They may be not understand everything you say, but God's Spirit is always present to prick even the conscience of a little child, and they will inherently know they were wrong.

Of course, being immature children, they *will* do it again, so be prepared for many repeats until they grow in understanding and eventually acquire both the habit and desire to please God and do what it right.

Meanwhile be vigilant and firm. If they return to quarreling, immediately banish them to different corners facing the wall until they are very bored and motivated to get along. It's amazing how fast they can learn to share when faced by the immediate threat of being punished and not having the opportunity to play at all.

> *Do all things without grumbling or disputing; that you may prove yourselves to be blameless and innocent, children of God above reproach in the midst of a crooked and perverse generation, among whom you appear as lights in the world.*
>
> *- Philippians 2:14-15*

## Tattling

**Constance:** My kids are always tattling on their siblings. They can't seem to discriminate between what is important and what isn't, so instructing them to report only the important stuff is useless. How do I handle tattling?

**Elizabeth:** It's true that young children cannot readily distinguish between what is important and what is not. I fully expect it to take years of parental effort to teach them to be discerning, but I know that's my job, so I roll up my sleeves and get to work. When I hear a complaint from one child about another, I don't just get annoyed and shoo him off with, "That's not important. Stop bothering me." Instead, I use it as an opportunity to *teach* the child to weigh and judge judiciously and to think and act appropriately.

Consider these examples:

**Child:** Whaaaa, Mom, he hit me!
**Me:** Are you hurt?
**Child:** No.
**Me:** Was he trying to hurt you?
**Child:** No.
**Me:** Did he "hit" you or did he just bump into you?
**Child:** He just bumped me.
**Me:** Did he do it on purpose to be mean? Or was it just an accident?
**Child:** It was an accident.
**Me:** What do you think I should do about him?
**Child:** I don't know.
**Me:** Should I spank him?
**Child:** *(beginning to feel a little guilty for tattling in an effort to get his sibling in trouble)* No.
**Me:** Don't report an accident like that if nobody is hurt and he didn't do it on purpose, okay? Now go play nicely and be careful.

Another example:

**Child:** Mom, he didn't put his shoes away.
**Me:** Did *you* put *your* shoes away?
**Child:** Yes.
**Me:** Are his shoes hurting anyone?
**Child:** No.
**Me:** Do you think I'll see his shoes where they don't belong?
**Child:** Yes.
**Me:** Then you really don't have to tell me, do you?
**Child:** No.

**Me:** *(pleasantly)* I do want you to tell me if he does something mean or dangerous, but you don't have to tell me about his shoes, ok?
**Child:** Okay.

Every circumstance is different and your response will also vary according to the age of the child. Try to get enough information to discern the motive behind the tattling and to figure out whether he was right in tattling, or not. Then direct the child to think properly, applying godly reasoning and values.

*For lack of wood the fire goes out, and where there is no whisperer, contention quiets down.*
*- Proverbs 26:20*

## Bickering

Teach your children to love their brothers and sisters. Later on they will treat their husbands and wives the way they treat their brothers and sisters now. In fact, the way your children treat their siblings is a preview of how they will likely treat every person they come in contact with the rest of their lives. How scary is that?!

But think about it. If they can't get along with their own siblings, who were all raised in the same house under the same parental teaching and value system, how will they ever get along with outsiders who have a myriad of personality types, standards, habits, beliefs, and customs?

If godliness is your goal for your children, it is also wise to consider that interaction between siblings provides every opportunity for your children to display their natural self-centered characters, providing you with the corresponding opportunity to teach and train them to deny their base nature and embrace and demonstrate God's nature instead.

The next time your children bicker, instead of becoming angry and looking simply for a quick fix to stop the annoyance, rejoice that another opportunity has presented itself for you to teach them what true Christianity is: to love God and to love others as you love yourself.

> *You shall not take vengeance, nor bear any grudge against the sons of your people, but you shall love your neighbor as yourself; I am the LORD.*
>
> *- Leviticus 19:18*

## Strife among Brothers

The "spreading of strife among brothers" is one of the seven things God hates, so if you detect any unkindness between siblings you must view it as meanness and hatred, and put a stop to it. You must motivate yourself to end all bickering, contentiousness, and strife among your children. It can be done, but it takes persistence and vigilance. When your children are very small, it is not difficult to stop bickering; just step in and correct. The heart of a small child will very often follow the child's actions, even if he does not fully understand it all. For example, if you diligently correct his selfishness by making him share, sharing will become a habit, and you will soon find that his heart has become inclined toward generosity.

When your children are quarreling, correct each of them according to what you know each did wrong. Don't be overly concerned about trying to learn the whole story. Don't try to make things work out perfectly fair. Life is not fair. Try to be just, but not "even" or "fair." Teach them that they must do what is right even if others wrong them. They should be taught to "go the extra mile" as Jesus taught us in *Matthew 5:41*. Watch for wrong attitudes toward each other. Continue working with all parties until they have a right attitude.

If you really want to stop all bickering (and you should), then listen, and stop it at the very first wrong tone of voice. Better yet, watch them closely and step in at the first angry look. But don't just tell them to stop. After you tell them to stop, watch and see that they do. If the bickering resumes, step in and give them specific instructions on how to act nicely and get along with one another. Discipline as needed.

Require them to apologize if they wronged each other. If they seem to be selectively slow learners in this area and continue to bicker, separate them, giving them each chores to do if they are old enough, or require them to sit nearby and do nothing until they are motivated to increase their comprehension.

One successful teaching technique I have used when a major dispute occurs is as follows: First I call the involved parties over. Then I ask one of them to begin to recount the incident. I may stop them periodically and ask the other if the things I am being told are true and accurate. I do not allow exaggeration or a negative attitude, only the simple, calmly told facts.

Then I go back to the very beginning and have both children act out exactly what was said and done. As they do this, they are required to act as they should have, not as they actually did. Of course, they never get to the dispute part. Next, they must again act out the incident, having the first offender repeat his first offense. The offended is then required to respond correctly, not as he actually did.

Disputes invariably begin with a very small action or word, escalating as wrong responses on both sides spur it on. If they are constantly bringing you tiny disagreements unnecessarily, try having them go through so much litigation (your questioning) that the next time they will try to settle out of court, by working things out peacefully themselves. Always look for opportunities to teach character.

There is one particular lecture I give my children when they bicker. I tell them with all sincerity that their brothers and sisters should always be their very best friends. Other friends will come and go (I insert examples from my life here), but siblings will always be family. They will always be there for us when we really need them. We need to understand the importance of acting with this in mind. We should always treat them better than we would anyone else and value them as we should.

I do my best to convince my children of these things. I remind them that bickering is one of the *"seven things"* the Lord hates.

> *There are six things which the LORD **hates,** yes, seven which are an **abomination** to Him: Haughty eyes, a lying tongue, and hands that shed innocent blood, a heart that devises wicked plans, feet that run rapidly to evil, a false witness who utters lies, and **one who spreads strife among brothers**.*
>
> *- Proverbs 6:16-19*

## Mass Bickering

**Norah:** With six young children, sometimes the bickering just gets out of control around here. I feel like I am rushing from one squabble to the next all day long, disciplining and trying to sort things out, to no avail. It just escalates until I'm ready to put them all up for adoption! What can I do?

**Elizabeth:** Once things get out of control, simply spot correcting after the fact doesn't really work. You have to start all over again, by restoring order in general, then keeping it. The way to do that is to group Tomato Stake.

So round everyone up and sit them all down and put them in "silent mode." Do not allow them to talk or even to look at each other, if it's too much for them to handle. Isolate them in separate corners or on separate chairs as needed. Discipline the troublemakers promptly if they remain slow to obey.

While they are practicing being silent and still, sit down yourself and decide what direction you want your family to go in next. Do you want to do schoolwork? Chores? Cooking? Fun? Maybe you'd like to spend an hour just "catching up."

Sometimes half of the problem is that we ourselves, don't know what we really want them to be doing, and they sense this. They know that no one is really at the helm, so they take advantage of the situation and cast off in whatever direction pleases them.

So decide what you would really like to have your children do next. Playing should probably be off the list and replaced with chores until they appreciate being allowed to play together and are motivated to play without bickering.

After you know where you want to be headed, outlast the kids until they are calmed down, out of the bickering mode, and bored enough to be motivated to cooperate. Then start giving directions to one child at a time, always having him return to you after finishing what you asked. Only send one child off at a time.

Keep them all with you as much as possible, while moving gradually in the direction you have decided to proceed that day. If you don't rush this, things should be back in order very soon. Keep things on track by not letting everyone go off in different directions and by returning any child who begins to bicker to silent mode and separation AS SOON AS the first disruption occurs.

*Hatred stirs up strife, but love covers all transgressions.*
*- Proverbs 10:12*

# fourteen

# INSIGHTFUL ISSUES

*And not only this, but we also exult in our tribulations, knowing that tribulation brings about perseverance; and perseverance, proven character; and proven character, hope; and hope does not disappoint, because the love of God has been poured out within our hearts through the Holy Spirit who was given to us.*

*- Romans 5:3-5*

## Miscellaneous Problems

In the two previous chapters, I've attempted to cover some very common childrearing concerns involving pride and sibling conflicts. Now in this last problem-solving chapter, I will be sharing advice regarding a collection of miscellaneous problems exemplifying a number of different character issues. Of course, these examples are in no way all-inclusive, and I will just be touching on the myriad of different scenarios that come up daily in the lives of real parents. If a problem you are facing is not specifically discussed here, I hope this chapter, and indeed this entire book, will encourage you to combine godly wisdom, Scriptural teaching, and inspired creativity, to find a solution. Hopefully, the principles that have been suggested throughout this book will be a valuable aid in helping you with this endeavor.

*He who neglects discipline despises himself, but he who listens to reproof acquires understanding.*

*- Proverbs 15:32*

## Consideration

**Corinna:** What is your philosophy and strategy for teaching children manners? How do you teach them to say please, thank you, to look adults in the eye, and so forth?

**Elizabeth:** If your children are under control and obedient, teaching manners is simple. Just tell them what you want them to do and remind them as needed. See that they do it without fail, at home or away. Starting young is always best. When they say, "I want a cookie," you respond with, "Say: 'May I please have a cookie.'" Every time you give them something, instruct them to say, "Thank you." Prior to visiting a restaurant, rehearse the rules: no getting out of their seats, no loud talking, etc. Never excuse them because they are just children, or because they are tired, or because it's "normal" for children to be rude and rambunctious. Communicate how you want them to act and require them to act that way.

When I teach manners, I try to carefully explain the principles behind them. In most instances, there are ways in which we demonstrate respect and consideration to one another. Our children are capable of understanding that. For example, I explain that we say, "Thank you," to show our gratitude to others. I remind my children to say, "Thank you," to someone who gives them a gift, whether or not they like the gift. I remind them that the person giving them the gift did it because they loved them, and cared about them and thought the gift would make them happy. I encourage them to be grateful that they have someone in their life who cares about them in this way.

I am always conducting running conversations with my children about things like this. Parents who teach manners as a sterile list of rules miss this exceptional opportunity to communicate the principles behind the rules of etiquette.

To review all the basics and obtain many ideas on what manners to teach children, and even how to teach the underlying principles of kindness and consideration, I recommend consulting *Miss Manners Guide to Excruciatingly Correct Behavior* and *Miss Manners Guide to Rearing Perfect Children* by Judith Martin. Both are very funny and informative books you can enjoy reading as a family.

> *Do not let kindness and truth leave you; bind them around your neck, write them on the tablet of your heart. So you will find favor and good repute in the sight of God and man.*
>
> \- *Proverbs 3:3-4*

## Dishonesty

**Hope:** Our seven-year-old is in a habit of lying. She's very good at it and I am not always sure whether she is telling the truth or not. She even lies to get others in trouble. What should we do? We've spanked for this, but it doesn't seem to change the behavior. I could really use some wisdom here.

**Elizabeth:** Any child you cannot trust completely needs to stay with you. If your child is lying, then you cannot trust her. I think you can plainly tell your seven-year-old what I just said. Then Tomato Stake her. Tell her she must stay with you until you can trust her again—a month, a year, or forever if that's what it takes. Because lying is a serious sin (another one of those seven things that God hates), there can be no excuse for even a child to lie. Do not believe that "all children lie now and then" or that "children really can't understand the difference between the truth and a lie." That is a lie itself!

A few of my toddlers tried lying once or twice, but that's it. Out of ten children, I only recall one or two instances where a post-toddler lied to me. Why? Are my children special? No, not at all. It is because from the outset, I hated lying, watched carefully for it, nipped it in the bud, and communicated my beliefs to the offenders about the subject. I taught them to hate it too.

If you cannot easily tell whether or not your child is lying, you may have to become a combo detective, interrogator, and mind reader to find out. When you quiz a child over a possible wrong, avoid tempting him to lie. A mother who is prone to losing her temper and letting her anger flare out of control, may soon find her children lying to avoid her wrath. So, remain calm and self-controlled.

If trying to identify a transgressor, it helps to question in a roundabout, non-threatening way. For example, one day I discovered pencil marks on the grout in my newly tiled bathroom. I did *not* bellow angrily, "WHO DID THIS?!" First, I called the most likely suspect and asked, in a normal tone of voice, "Have you used the bathroom lately? Did you notice anything unusual in there? Did you take your pencil with you? Did you use it on anything?"

I gently questioned each suspect on my list and soon I had a pretty good idea who was innocent. I detained those I thought might be guilty and questioned them individually once again. Before long, I was quite certain I knew the identity of the bathroom artist.

Finally, I asked this child directly, "Did you color on the grout in the bathroom?" An evasive answer told me with certainty that I had the culprit who, with a little more gentle persuasion, then confessed and was disciplined. (With some obviously guilty children, it helps if you prompt them by telling them, "Say 'Yes, I did it Mom.'")

I never got upset or angry. I continued questioning until I felt confident that I knew who was lying. Then I focused on getting that child to admit it and own up to it. I disciplined reasonably to motivate the child not to repeat the misbehavior. I lectured to instill correct values, and then I tightened my Tomato Staking to head off a future reoccurrence.

Instilling the value of honesty daily around the home is the most effective way to head off lying, but if your child has already acquired the habit, then you also MUST keep your child with you to help him overcome it.

*A false witness will not go unpunished, and he who tells lies will perish.*

*- Proverbs 19:9*

## Forgetfulness

**Pamela:** How do I teach my seven-year-old son to remember to do things without being told each step of the way? He forgets to change his socks and underwear unless I am in his room telling him. He forgets to turn off the lights when he leaves a room. He does not clean up the toothpaste he splattered on the counter while brushing his teeth. He forgets to load his dishes in the dishwasher. I tell him to keep his hands in his lap, but soon he is fiddling with items on the table. What's the remedy?

**Elizabeth:** In the case of chores, try adding a little motivating consequence to reminders—make him start all over when he forgets. For example:

**Him:** *(he brushes his teeth and comes downstairs.)*
**You:** Did you brush your teeth?
**Him:** Yes! *(big smile)*
**You:** Great! They look nice and white. Now, did you clean up the sink after you were done?
**Him:** Ahhh, I think so. *(which tells you he probably didn't, or didn't do it very well)*

**You:** Go back upstairs and double-check to see if you did. Make sure it's really clean, then come back down and give me a report.

**Him:** Okay, Mom.

Putting him to the trouble of returning to repeat the chores all over again will motivate him to try harder in the future to do it right the first time. Repeat this with everything he routinely "forgets" or fails to perform satisfactorily.

For things he forgets to do right while you are beside him watching, like your "hands on the lap" example, the most effective cure is ambushing. Train yourself to be observant each time you give a command or direction, noting whether he continues to obey you or "forgets." Be ready to ambush him with immediate and motivating correction. Be consistent and he will soon learn not to "forget."

*Acquire wisdom! Acquire understanding! Do not forget, nor turn away from the words of my mouth.*

*- Proverbs 4:5*

## Gratefulness

Gratitude makes rejoicing easy. Cultivating a spirit of gratefulness also makes it difficult to sink into depression. Discover reasons to be thankful in *every* situation. Train yourself to do this and teach your children likewise. Require them to express their thanks whenever possible.

The everyday, often minute situations are the most important. If your child complains about a sibling, for example, ask him to list several things he is grateful for in that sibling. Do not allow grumbling or whining—from your children or yourself.

Although your aim is a constant spirit of gratefulness, one thing we have done in our home, to get the ball rolling and keep it rolling, is to have each child keep a "Blessing Book," a journal expressing thanksgiving for God's bountiful daily blessings. Older children keep their Blessing Books themselves in a blank notebook or on the computer, while the younger children, unable yet to spell or write, tell Mom their blessings of the day and she records them. At week's end, we share some of our special blessings within our family and with our Christians friends who do the same.

> *In everything give thanks; for this is God's will for you in Christ Jesus.*
>
> *- I Thessalonians 5:18*

## Impulsiveness

**Trina:** What can I do to calm my son's impulsiveness? He is seven years old and his heart is good—he really wants to obey. But he does things impulsively, without thinking. Here is a brief list of impulsive things he did just yesterday afternoon:

- Threw a Little Tykes bike, breaking off a wheel.
- Bounced a wet dishrag off the ceiling.
- Planted his foot in the baby's face.
- Leapt into his startled sister's lap while she was studying on the couch.

When I ask why he does such things, he says, "I don't know. I just wasn't thinking." He doesn't act out of defiance, but rather out of playful impulsiveness, without thinking of the consequences. What I can do to help him to develop self-restraint and prudence?

**Elizabeth:** There is only one cure for impulsiveness—vigilant Tomato Staking. Monitor the impulsive child closely, requiring him to stop and think *before* an impulsive misdeed. If he is on the verge of an impulsive act, call out "STOP" or "FREEZE." Then, grill him with thought-provoking questions. For example:

"STOP. Do you think that's a wise thing to do? Do you think that's the right thing to do? Do you think that is a safe thing to do? What if something goes wrong? Would Dad do that? What would others think if they saw you acting so foolishly?"

Do not be annoyed every time you have to correct. This is part of his inborn nature, which is not an excuse, but a motivation for you to work all the harder training him to overcome it.

Recognize that you are in for the long haul, and you must persist for as long as it takes, even if that means years. When you see improvement, be sure to lavish praise and encouragement. Help him to see you as an ally in this fight to overcome impulsiveness, not just as a nagging mom.

*Every prudent man acts with knowledge, but a fool displays folly.*

*- Proverbs 13:16*

## Modesty

**Valerie:** When do children become modest?

**Elizabeth:** As soon as you teach them to. When my children are old enough to get dressed without help or use the bathroom unassisted, I start teaching them to be modest. I simply say, "We don't display our bodies; we dress in private." They learn to shut the door when dressing or using the bathroom and to knock before they enter a bedroom or bathroom. With several boys sharing the same bedroom, I don't expect them to take turns dressing, but I do expect them to avoid making a spectacle of themselves. They all know when to turn and look the other way.

I did once catch one of my younger boys before bedtime, dancing around the room in his birthday suit in front of his little brothers, trying to be funny. (His older brother discreetly alerted me as to what was going on.) The earnest spanking he received convinced him that immodesty isn't funny. There's never been a repeat.

The teaching we apply is Biblically-based and stresses that God greatly favors modesty and so, unless they are married (a husband is one with his wife, so there is no need for modesty between them), they are to be modest. They are not to be running around half dressed.

Girls especially must be taught that their clothing can be immodest if it is overly revealing or sensuous, appealing to the appetites. I explain that they should dress in a way that attracts others to their faces and their countenance, not their figures.

I teach these things as the need arises and I do it very naturally in the course of everyday living. For example, I remember visiting a park one day with one of my girls when a scantily clad woman happened by. After she left, I quietly asked my young daughter if she had noticed her. She had, and observed, "She wasn't very modest." I asked if she'd like to dress that way and she said, "No!" Her response pleased me greatly.

Of course, in enforcing the idea of modesty, I cite the story of Noah's son Ham, who stumbled upon his father in a drunken and immodest state. That son didn't avert his eyes or discreetly keep the matter to himself, but instead hastened to tell his brothers.

The result was that Ham's descendents were cursed forever. The other brothers covered their father without looking themselves and were blessed in the end. The lesson is simple and clear: if you see something immodest, quickly look away, then act as though you saw nothing and forget it.

*But Shem and Japheth took a garment and laid it upon both their shoulders and walked backward and covered the nakedness of their father; and their faces were turned away, so that they did not see their father's nakedness.*
*- Genesis 9:23*

## Resistance

**Selma:** In our home, one goal we always aim for is prompt obedience. But what do you do when your school-aged child says, "But I don't want to…?" Until now, my response has been, "I didn't ask if you *wanted* to, I *told* you to do it." But then, the tears start. Is there a better way to handle this, or will this be part of the adjustment process as I "retrain" my child?

**Elizabeth:** Yes, the tears could be a reaction to your change in disciplining style. Perhaps he was used to getting away with slow obedience and poor attitudes in the past, and he's disappointed to find that he cannot do so now. But still, don't let it slide. Train your child to respond correctly. When he says, "But I don't want to," pleasantly reply, "Say, 'Okay Mom.'" If he still resists, be more serious and insist that he say, "Okay Mom," and then does what you asked. When your child responds verbally in the affirmative, it actually helps him to obey, and to do so with a right attitude. If the tears still start, remain calm and take the time to see that he dries them up and responds pleasantly before you move on.

Remember never to engage in verbal argument with an older child. He should know that the subject is not negotiable. An older child may politely question a request *after* he shows a willingness to obey with a good attitude.

*Children, obey your parents in the Lord, for this is right.*
*- Ephesians 6:1*

# Responsibility

Assigning chores has always been employed by parents to teach responsibility. I, too, assign chores for this purpose, but in ways that represent a departure from the usual model of heavily scheduled lists and strictly divided duties.

My approach is different because of the problems posed by the traditional way. I began to notice early on that assigning specific chores to specific children soon resulted in selfishness, laziness, and dissention. Each child focused exclusively on *his* list and was extremely reluctant to help anyone else, thus risking the chance he might do one iota more work than his own list specified.

So, I devised a different method that aims more at teaching helpfulness, flexibility, and true responsibility, than just at getting the chores done. Instead of assigning specific chores to specific children, I keep my own, continually changing list of duties, and assign them according to age and ability *as the need arises.* I assume the role of a hands-on director and supervisor, rather than assigning permanent chores and being disappointed when things go awry and I wind up playing referee and slave-driver all day.

Although I am opposed to using a strict schedule unless absolutely necessary, I do follow a general routine. It works best for me to have the bulk of the chores done in the morning, so that's when I look over my list and give out assignments. I may give each child a list for that morning, but I make a pointed effort to change that list daily to keep everyone on his toes. There is a continual rotation of tasks and frequent, unexpected new jobs assigned that are not on anyone's list.

I continually repeat the following: "Your job is to do anything that needs to be done," and, "When you are done, come and ask me what to do next," and, "If you see something that needs doing, do it," and "Do your job *and* a little bit more."

As our older children have aged, I have been very pleased with the results. They rarely need more than the occasional assignment. They seem to have a well-rounded idea of what is involved in keeping a home and they all pitch in without being told. I even find them voluntarily helping me with my organizing! "Mom, do you need anything from the store?" or "Mom, would you like me to get the younger kids started folding the laundry?" are among the questions I hear routinely. I couldn't be happier.

> *Two are better than one because they have a good return for their labor. For if either of them falls, the one will lift up his companion. But woe to the one who falls when there is not another to lift him up. Furthermore, if two lie down together they keep warm, but how can one be warm alone? And if one can overpower him who is alone, two can resist him. A cord of three strands is not quickly torn apart.*
>
> *- Ecclesiastes 4:9-12*

## Self-Control

**Philana:** I'm trying to homeschool a child who fidgets—incessantly. He's not an unusually hyperactive child in general; he just doesn't seem to be using any self-control during school time.

He is supposed to be writing, and I notice he is messing with his pencil sharpener. I tell him to put it down. He does, and then two minutes later, he is tapping the pencil on his forehead or poking it into his ear. I tell him to stop. In a few minutes he is pushing against the computer desk door, a no-no. Meanwhile, he is perpetually wiggling in his chair, often falling onto the floor. Soon, he's messing with the pencil sharpener again. Should I be endlessly reminding him all day to stop? Should I swat? What?

**Elizabeth:** First, you must seat this child right next to you while you are schooling, not across the table. Lay your paddle on the table between you as a visual aid. Begin like this:

**Mom:** Do you see this paddle?

**Child:** Yes.

**Mom:** I'm tired of reminding you not to touch, fidget, wiggle, or to rock in your chair. From now on, I'm going to use the paddle to help you remember. Do you understand me?

**Child:** Yes, Mom.

**Mom:** What are some of the things I'm always telling you not to do?

**Child:** Playing with my eraser?

**Mom:** Yes. What else?

**Child:** Getting off my chair?

**Mom:** Yes. What else?

**Child:** Scribbling instead of doing my math?

**Mom:** Yes, and I'm sure you can think of a lot of other things, so I'm not going to remind you. I'm just going to use the paddle. Do you understand me?

**Child:** Yes.

*(Two minutes later child begins rocking in his chair.)*

**Mom:** Get up and put your hands on the table. *(SWAT!)* Now sit back down and go back to your work.

*(Three minutes later child begins to poke his pencil through his buttonhole.)*

**Mom:** Get up and put your hands on the table. *(SWAT!)* Sit down and start working.

*(Five minutes later child begins tapping the table leg with his foot.)*

**Mom:** Get up and put your hands on the table. *(SWAT! SWAT!)* Sit down and work.

As soon as he realizes that he controls whether or not he gets a swat, he will start improving. If he laughs, or exhibits a bad attitude, apply an "I Mean Business" spanking. Remember, this will not work if you are not being very consistent, so you MUST train yourself to notice every little thing. Decide what degree of fidgeting is acceptable, taking into consideration the personality of your child, then correct for everything that is excessive. He is probably not even aware of his excessive movements and he needs you to bring them to his attention and insist he control them.

> *And being aroused, He rebuked the wind and said to the sea, "Hush, be still." And the wind died down and it became perfectly calm.*
>
> *- Mark 4:39*

## Silliness

**Jennifer:** My almost six-year-old son loves being silly and drawing attention to himself, and he just doesn't know when to stop. For example, at choir practice he was sitting with the other children and another boy said, "This kid eats his shoe," pointing to my son. My son responded with, "I eat my underwear, too," and they all started laughing. Soon afterwards, he saw another child dancing around acting goofy and, of course, he joined in and began imitating her to get the other kids to laugh at him too.

In both cases, I quickly discouraged him, but he keeps doing this kind of thing. How do I stop this behavior? I want him to have fun, but some of this seems inappropriate.

**Elizabeth:** This, of course, is just another symptom of typical childish self-centeredness. He wants to draw attention to himself and has stumbled upon an effective way to do it. If it's just occasional silliness, then I'd be watching for it and stopping it BEFORE it goes too far (which is usually right at the beginning).

Teaching has to accompany this. Point out to your child that he should be paying attention to others, not trying to get them to pay attention to him. It will help if you enable your child to understand the difference between being laughed *with* and being laughed *at*. Work to instill in him a desire to appear (and indeed *be*) mature and wise, not foolish and goofy.

These are things that you need to be teaching all day, every day, not just once in a while when he makes a major fool out of himself. Meanwhile, do correct him every time he acts in this unflattering manner.

*My son, if your heart is wise, my own heart also will be glad;*
*And my inmost being will rejoice, when your lips speak what is right.*

*- Proverbs 23:15-16*

## Thriftiness

We do not give allowances. Our children are not given personal money they can spend any way they wish. We do not encourage everyone to think of themselves as separate entities with separate bank accounts, earnings, and expenses. Instead, we teach our children to view finances as part of the makeup of our family as a whole. Then, employing our mentoring style of Tomato Staking, we educate them regarding the wise management of money as they participate with us in the management of our *family* finances.

In our home, we do not budget our income in the usual manner. That is to say, we do not determine our fixed expenses, set aside that amount, then save and tithe a determined amount and spend the rest. That seems to be the most commonly suggested plan and it often winds up with everyone living on the very edge of financial safety or disaster.

Instead, we begin by considering how we can *save* on *every* purchase. If we are coming up short, we cut expenses and look for ways to increase income. If we have excess, we do not look for ways to spend it frivolously, but rather ways to invest that will benefit our family or others. We may determine it would be best to save it for the future.

The first thing we teach our children regarding spending is to determine if they really need something. Then, is it a good thing? Is it a good price? For a non-necessity, we consider whether it would be a profitable (spiritually or financially) and affordable purchase, or whether we are better off without it.

We don't pay our children for household chores, since it is their *responsibility* to do these things. We all live here, so we all do the work here. No one pays Mom to cook the meals or change the diapers.

We teach our children to help others without expecting payment. We never let them take payment from their grandparents or those in need. We make every effort to teach them to be generous, without neglecting the financial responsibilities that God has specifically given them. In *Matthew 15:3-6*, Jesus criticized the religious leaders of His day for giving all their money to the church instead of to their own needy parents, so that is our example.

We don't allow debt of any kind. Several years ago we went through the entire Bible and looked up every verse we could find having anything to do with debt, borrowing, lending, interest, usury, and so forth. We found that, lo and behold, the Bible has nothing good to say about borrowing. The main thought that has motivated us to remain debt-free is the knowledge that *"the borrower becomes the lender's slave."* I would highly recommend that you teach your children to live a debt free life.

> *The rich rules over the poor, and the borrower becomes the lender's slave.*
>
> *- Proverbs 22:7*

## Part V

# The Parent's Part

*Now for this very reason also, applying all diligence, in your faith supply moral excellence, and in your moral excellence, knowledge; and in your knowledge, self-control, and in your self-control, perseverance, and in your perseverance, godliness; and in your godliness, brotherly kindness, and in your brotherly kindness, love.*

- II Peter 1:5-7

# fifteen

# Fixing Ourselves First

*Scorners set a city aflame, but wise men turn away anger.*

*- Proverbs 29:8*

## Training Mom

We are under a divine mandate to train our children. So far, I've written an entire book about how to do this, and now I'm close to the end and it's time to face up to the biggest challenge of all—training ourselves. We can try to follow all the discipline and Tomato Staking rules, watch for character problems, ambush, outlast, lecture, and so on and so forth, but if we are hypocrites ourselves in the way we live and in our own attitudes, we will eventually have serious problems with our children, probably sooner than later.

We may get outward obedience, but we will lose our children's hearts, and we may indeed permanently hinder their relationship with Christ. So stop now and clean up your act, so that you can be the mom you want to be, leading your beloved children to godliness of both action and heart, and ultimately to a life of love and devotion to God. *"You hypocrite, first take the log out of your own eye, and then you will see clearly to take the speck out of your brother's eye." - Matthew 7:5*

I'm not going to grill you about habits and deeds here; I think most of you know which of those types of things you need to change in your life and how to do it. (Just do it.) Rather, I'm going to skip right to the issue that is by far the most damaging to your relationship with your children—the issue of Mom's ability or inability to control her own emotions.

If you have a problem in this area, I know that your conscience is smiting you right now. You know that I am speaking about irritability, frustration, and anger. If we are unable to control our own tempers, how can we teach our children to control theirs? We feel guilty for even trying. Be assured that all our good childrearing efforts will be tragically undermined if we are unkind, unfair, and angry in the way we treat our children.

On the other hand, if we learn to control our own emotions, we will be far better equipped to teach our children how to control theirs. I hope you will be encouraged here by the testimony of other moms who are working on this same issue and will glean some tidbits that will be keys enabling you to achieve control over your own spirit, giving you the ability to successfully apply all the other teachings in this book.

> *...do not exasperate your children, that they may not lose heart.*
>
> *- Colossians 3:21*

## Mom's Emotions

**Leonie:** I have a sad heart tonight.... I just lost a showdown with my five dear children who have *not* been getting on well lately at all. I'm constantly battling bad attitudes. They snap and snarl at each other at the slightest provocation. No soft answers, no patience, no mercy toward each other. You get the picture.

Now, here's what makes me *really* sad. I'm sure this all comes from me! I'm always on the verge of exploding. I am angry, I yell and lash out.

When I talked to my ten-year-old son tonight, he cried and said his heart is "full of anger and ugliness and it keeps spilling out." I cried too, as I considered that my sin has created the same feeling in him. He has watched me and "learned" how to react to stress and demands by snapping at others!

Is there a way to undo this damage? I *really* want the joy of God in my family. How do I become a calm, serene, cheerful, *joyful* mommy? Help me please.

**Elizabeth:** I used to be very easily frustrated, so I can truly relate to your problem. Things were far worse when my oldest ones were little, because I didn't know how to parent effectively. Things were often bordering on chaos, and predictably, my frustrations were often near the explosion point. Then, I changed my parenting ways and the situation improved immensely.

Once I knew what to do when my children misbehaved, I wasn't nearly so annoyed by their misbehavior. But, alas, other things besides the children still annoyed and irritated me, and my agitation still impacted the entire family.

For example, I would get all agitated over something as small as an accidental spill or a dropped can of soup. I'd voice my displeasure with "Shoot," then let my anger swell, as I moaned, *"Life is so rough,"* and *"Why is it always me?"* and *"Why can't anything ever go right?"* and so on ad nauseam. If the kids were around, I'd let my anger spill over on them too.

Then my face would turn red with embarrassment and I'd tear up as I started to feel guilty for losing my temper, snapping at my children, and thinking such selfish, ungrateful thoughts. Finally I'd end this emotional ordeal in a state of depression by beating myself up for being a complete failure as a Christian, a wife, a mother, and even a person. I'd repent and pray that it would never happen again, but, of course it would, and I'd repeat the cycle again and again.

Finally, I changed my perspective. I decided to view my irritability as a serious sin, not just an unfortunate personality flaw. I decided to view losing my temper as *totally* unacceptable and *completely* forbidden. Instead of seeking to "improve," I determined to "quit." I changed to viewing anger as *poison,* not just as a small, bothersome, bad habit. Big difference.

Henceforth, I began to ponder this "poison" many times a day and prepare for it, instead of waiting until a frustrating incident came along, producing its impulsive response. I determined that anger or irritation was NOT AN OPTION, period.

My resolve was to be alert and ready, not passively doing nothing until sin was knocking at the door. I purposed that despite anything that might occur, I'd find some way to maintain control. I WOULD NOT become angry!

I still dropped that can of soup now and then, but I was alert to my responses and each time chose one that was different from the one I'd grown accustomed to. As that can slipped out of my grasp, I would think, *"Relax. It's just a can of soup. Getting upset is ridiculous, ungodly, and WRONG, and it is NOT AN OPTION. It's just a can of soup. So what if it hits my foot or makes a mess? I'm going to smile, just take care of things, and move on."*

What a help that was! Yes, I still occasionally messed up. After all, I'd had many years of practice being easily annoyed. But I could immediately see a big difference and I kept at it. To make this work, I had to keep pondering my newfound abhorrence of anger. I had to keep thinking, *"Getting angry is NOT AN OPTION,"* and *"This is NOT something to get upset about,"* and *"I will deal this some other way."*

Within six months, I defeated the habit of being constantly annoyed and irritated. To be released of that burden is gloriously liberating.

So how are things now? Well, last week I was opening the lid on my chili at Wendy's and splashed chili all over my blouse. What was my reaction? Well, fifteen or twenty years ago, anger and a *"Why me?"* attitude would have been the response. This time, none of that even crossed my mind.

It really did not occur to me to be angry. Instead, my mind analyzed the mishap and dealt with it: *"Hmmm, those are unsightly grease spots. I wonder what will be the best way to get this off. What would I have done if this had happened on our way out to that meeting? Would I have tried to wash it out in the restroom or what? I'm sure thankful it happened now instead."* Actually, it was almost amusing the way I silently thought through the whole scenario without really reacting emotionally at all. How liberating this new spirit is!

My message to you is this: You CAN change. I did. You will have to be your own parent though, and train yourself. If you know how to train your children, that will help you train yourself. Are you focusing on the details? Are you nipping things in the bud—taking care of the *"little foxes"* that are *"ruining the vineyard"? (Song of Solomon 2:15 - "Catch the foxes for us, the little foxes that are ruining the vineyards….")*

You must cultivate and ponder a HATRED for anger, be vigilantly on guard for its earliest signs of emergence, and be prepared to immediately *overcome evil with good* by replacing angry reactions with calmness and godly, right thoughts.

Watch yourself closely, raise your standards, and train yourself to be godly, just as you want your children to be godly. Remember that your children can and will change as you do, IF you do.

> *Therefore, putting aside all malice and all guile and hypocrisy and envy and all slander, like newborn babes, long for the*

> *pure milk of the Word, that by it you may grow in respect to salvation, if you have tasted the kindness of the Lord.*
> *- I Peter 2:1-3*

## A Critical Spirit

**Leslie:** Critical and mean. These unpleasant adjectives describe both me and my daughter. I realize now that I am not a very nice mommy. My frustrated heart taints my spirit and echoes in my voice.

I like my children most of the time. They are a joy and I'm happy being their mom. I know that there is no greater calling. But sadly, I am aware that the destructive attitudes I hold so frequently have done significant damage to them. My daughter, now seven, is highly critical and possesses a sharp tongue—qualities that I strongly suspect were learned from me. I am praying hard for God to work both on me and my daughter.

My question is this, do I pray and let God work, or do I discipline her for her harsh words? She has been an exemplary child for the most part—quick to obey, cheerful, diligent, and kind—until recently. But now I'm noticing her mouth becoming sarcastic and snide and I hate it. Oh, Elizabeth, help!

**Elizabeth:** Should you "pray and let God work"? WHAT!? I mean, what exactly are you expecting God to do? God has put you in authority over your child for the purpose of raising a godly child. So don't expect Him to take over the job He gave to you.

He has already convicted you that *you* are the source of your daughter's critical spirit and that you need to change. So get going. First, start obeying Him. Stop your own sharp tongue! Stop the criticism. Make this your top priority.

Remember what Proverbs says about an excellent wife: *"She opens her mouth in wisdom, and the teaching of kindness is on her tongue."*

- *Proverbs 31:26.* Watch yourself, and instead of criticism, give encouragement and praise. If you can't be kind, generous, or sympathetic, say nothing. Above all, train yourself *not* to be angry.

Should you discipline your daughter, even though you are not yet perfect? Absolutely! Apply whatever discipline is needed to correct her tongue, but make sure she understands that it is her heart that is wrong and needs changing. Help her to "think" differently. Help her to replace her discouraging, mean words with kind, edifying ones.

A critical spirit is often rooted in pride or ungratefulness. Tell her plainly that you intend to discipline her every time you hear her critical mouth. Tell her that after she is disciplined, she will be required to think of three sincere compliments to give the person she criticized. Make her apologize sincerely, if she criticizes face to face.

Declare war on this bad spirit in both of you. Don't let it continue to rule your lives. Be thankful that she is only seven and can be changed with consistency and diligence.

You can change too, but since you have no one to Tomato Stake you, it will be harder. Know that you are not helpless; God has given Christians victory over sin and you can master your critical spirit. Keep the future of your daughter in mind as your motivator.

Should you pray for your daughter? Of course, but if you discipline her while you are exempting yourself, don't expect much change; expect to create further bitterness in her.

**Follow-up from Leslie:** Thank you for your direct reply. I needed that. If we can't count on fellow Christian women to rebuke us, imagine the road we would go down! It's a new day! God has truly, truly given me more joy and peace in the last week than ever before. I'm thrilled.

I don't think I realized what a unpleasant place I was creating around here with my raised voice and critical tone. My daughter is responding wonderfully to a mama who corrects her criticisms in a gentle, loving way.

Thank you Elizabeth for correcting me. Because Christ is my Savior, I have the desire and the power to choose good over evil. Patience and anger were attributes I was *choosing* and these are certainly not fruits of the Spirit. Elizabeth, you were right on the money when you said the Lord has done His part in convicting me. I had to *choose* Him and His fruit rather than choosing the evils of anger and malice. Thank you Elizabeth!

> *But thanks be to God that though you were slaves of sin, you became obedient from the heart to that form of teaching to which you were committed, and having been freed from sin, you became slaves of righteousness.*
>
> *- Romans 6:17,18*

## Cultivating Love and Joy

**Birdie:** All my life I dreamed of the joys of being a mom. I wanted to dance with my children, sing silly songs, paint, roll Play-Doh, and blow bubbles. My children would have fun, learn much along the way, and be members of a happy, harmonious home.

Unfortunately, for various reasons, I have not attained what I wished and am wondering if there is still hope. If I were to start suddenly being "fun," my oldest daughter (three years old) would look at me as if I had grown a second head. I want desperately to find joy in playing with her and being her mommy, without surrendering the right of family discipline.

I honestly believe that my daughter's behavior would be better if I were less tense and more enjoyable to be around. How do I engage in simple fun with her and still get the baby fed, do the laundry and cooking, and perform all my other required chores? I just don't know how to fit it all in. Any thoughts?

**Elizabeth:** Some moms are great "kid people." I am not. I'm not good at playing house with the girls or trucks and cars with the boys. However, I excel at smiling when a child shows me his latest creation. I am good at hoisting a toddler eager for a hug. I show frequent flashes of humor and am good at conferring on any child a portion of my undivided attention. You need not commit a fixed portion of the day to deliberate play or "quality time." Every moment spent with your children should be quality time, even when disciplining.

Just a minute or so of attention will greatly please a child and confer love and security. For this, they will usually come to you without being beckoned. When they do, stop your routine and make yourself physically and emotionally available. Smile, answer their questions, give them your undivided attention, and then, when they have been satisfied, return to your work.

If they are bored and you are occupied, stop and give some pleasant direction for their next activity. If possible, include them in what you are doing, especially when they show spontaneous interest. Most small children love to be Mommy's little helper, so let them help you whenever you can.

Consider this real life example that I recently jotted down. My youngest (two years old at the time) approached me as I was working at my computer, and with big eyes and an excited smile, showed me a little Lego man in his hand. I stopped, smiled, hugged him, and said, "Wow! What's that?" He smiled and responded with "I am stinky!" Well that gave me a good laugh.

**Me:** *(still smiling)* "Oh, really? Did someone send you to me?"
**Him:** "Noooooo."
**Me:** *(enthusiastically)* Did you come here all by yourself? *(I'm teaching here.)*
**Him:** *(nodding excitedly)* Yeah!

**Me:** "Oh good! Say 'Yes,' not 'yeah.'" *(Still pleasantly teaching.)*

**Him:** *(smiling)* "Yes!"

**Me:** *(still cheerful and smiling)* "Good, that sounds much nicer. Now lay down here, so I can change you."

This exchange might seem trifling, but it reflects the importance of ENJOYING your children, extending your love, attention, and approval when they come to you all those precious little times throughout the day.

And, by the way, when he did not lay down right away, I had no problem switching to a more serious tone and saying, "Lay down right now so momma can change you." You do not have to sacrifice discipline to have a loving relationship with your child.

*For the LORD takes pleasure in His people;*

*- Psalms 149:4*

# sixteen

# OLDER CHILDREN

*Let no one look down on your youthfulness, but rather in speech, conduct, love, faith and purity, show yourself an example of those who believe.*
*- I Timothy 4:12*

## But Will They Just Be Faking?

While *Raising Godly Tomatoes* is primarily aimed at younger children, I have had so many requests for "something about older children" that I feel compelled to at least mention them briefly here, and share some of my parenting thoughts in their regard.

When I only had young ones, I intensely wanted them to *really* love the Lord and to do everything out of a love for Him, not just because I was making them. But yet they were really too young to comprehend deep spiritual matters. I couldn't really sit them down and have a heart-to-heart with them about my love for God and the reasons for my faith. Finally, I realized that, FIRST, I had to confront what was in front of me, a small child with wrong habits and bad attitudes. I changed my focus from thinking I had to first *persuade* them to love God (and so do what was right), to believing that for the moment, my responsibility was just to *train* them to do what was right, period. I would trust the faith to come later.

Of course, I didn't rely on training alone for the long term. *As* I trained them, I also showed them God through my life, and as soon as they were able to understand my words, I began diligently teaching them all I knew about God and His ways. This is the entire gist of the Tomato Staking lifestyle: continually sharing your faith, love, and knowledge of God with your children daily as you include them in your life, inviting them to walk with you as Adam, Noah, and Enoch walked with God.

Most of my children seemed to have made a transition from habitual obedience to genuine faith and a personal desire to please God, some time in their very early teens. Before that, they obeyed God because they had been trained to and because they believed in *us*.

Eventually, I observed that they were consciously trying to obey God because *they* wanted to and because they believed in *God*. Perhaps the changeover was gradual, or all at once in a specific "salvation experience"—I don't really know, but by the time their personal commitment to Christ warranted baptism, I believe they had all been true followers of Christ for some time, even if they could not identify a specific date of conversion.

*So then, those who had received his word were baptized; and there were added that day about three thousand souls.*
*- Acts 2:41*

## Godly and Prompt Resolution

It would take me another entire book and more to write all my thoughts about teens, but there is one key to a good relationship with them that I feel compelled to emphasize. It is the matter of resolving whatever differences you have with them *as soon as possible*. Although vows are taken very seriously by God, *Numbers 30:5* tells us that a parent was given by the God the right to nullify a foolish vow made by his daughter, but *only* if he acted promptly. In fact, it had to be in the same day he became aware that the vow had been made. Similarly, I believe conflicts between you and your children are extremely serious matters, and it is very important to fix any misunderstanding or resolve any differences you have with your child *"in the day you hear of it."* Perhaps, unlike a vow, resolution can be put off until later, but the damage the conflict has caused will be far more serious, and the resolution much harder to come by.

By the time my children are of this older age, I haven't had to spank or tightly Tomato Stake them for a long time. If an issue comes up, we talk. Usually, if I have a complaint about their behavior or attitude, a brief discussion is all that is needed. If they have a complaint about a sibling, they come to me and we talk. Then, if I think it's needed, I talk to the sibling. Or, if I think the complainant needs to make some change, I encourage the change and how to make it.

If they have a complaint against me (example: "I always get all the work around here…"), then I sit down with the complainant and we talk, politely and considerately, until the issue is resolved. If they don't come to me, but I think there may be something bothering them, I go to them.

That last paragraph is the key. No matter what the issue is, you must talk UNTIL THE ISSUE IS RESOLVED. I suppose that's one of my ongoing life mottos, enshrined in the verse, *"Don not let the sun go down on your anger."* If the anger is your child's anger, then it is still your obligation to resolve the conflict *"in the day that you hear of it."*

Now what do I mean by "resolved"? Surely, not by forcing your will on your stubborn child. Nor do you strike a bargain or cave in to keep the peace. I mean that you discuss the issue until you agree on what pleases God, the right course of action, and what godly attitudes are required. You both must do right and you both must agree. No quitting until the issue is brought to a godly resolution. This will preserve your relationship with your teens more than anything else.

*Be angry, and yet do not sin; do not let the sun go down on your anger....*

*- Ephesians 4:26*

# Turning Around an Older Child

At the time of this writing, my youngest child is seven and my oldest is twenty-seven, with all ten spaced about two years apart. So seven of them are teen-aged or above. Yet, I have never experienced any teen rebellion, raging hormones, drug or promiscuity problems, or...well...ANY significant problems. Really!

I've never experienced a heated argument with even one of them. So, while I can't speak from the actual experience of turning a rebellious teen around, what I can do is tell you briefly a few things I believe are important in raising older ones, and what a parent ought to do to restore a wayward child.

Older children are not, in many ways, all that different from younger ones. After all, these really are the very same people you knew as babies, toddlers, and grade-schoolers. If your relationship was close back then, it should be close now. If it was close then and isn't close now, something has changed that didn't have to change.

Your children should have gradually been mentored and nurtured into competent, trustworthy young people of faith, whom you respect as friends. They should not have remained immature and unthinking individuals, either mentally or spiritually, who must be given directions, then compelled to do it against their will.

I reject the claim that at the age of twelve or thirteen, all children have a "need" to be more independent. That's not it. We all have that urge at all ages, don't we? If it seems stronger at one time than another, I would suspect that we are really talking more about a breakdown in your relationship than independence. Something else is going on that needs to be resolved:

Perhaps you have been too controlling or oppressive.
Perhaps your child has too much freedom and has come to believe he is entitled to more rights than he should possess.
Perhaps there is a destructive, evil influence coming from school, friends, church, books, TV, or music, etc.
Perhaps your child nurses a gripe against you that has never been resolved (bitterness).
Perhaps your child has never learned to respect you in the first place.
Perhaps you haven't treated your child with due respect.
Perhaps you have not instilled loyalty or a love for "family."

If your older child displays such a belligerent, rebellious spirit, examine this list to see if any of it applies. Keep looking into these possibilities and perhaps others, until you discover the root problem.

Remember my insistence that you MUST settle all conflicts COMPLETELY and as soon as possible? That's probably where you messed up. Somewhere along the line, you let your child stomp off in a huff and you didn't call him back, assess the problem, and fix it. Then it happened again and again, and soon you became alienated.

More than likely, you have not only lost his loyalty, but he has acquired replacements for you—friends, perhaps teachers, or others that he looks up to—who probably are hostile or indifferent to your values and beliefs. The only remaining alternative is to try to start over.

Where do you start? That's easy. With you. Reread the "*Fixing Ourselves First*" chapter and take it to heart. If you've been an angry parent, stop, and apologize to your child. If you've been a hypocrite in any other way, repent (which includes changing) and apologize for that too.

Only when you are committed to obeying God yourself will your child be inspired to do the same. Humble yourself, admit your failings, ask forgiveness, and then start being the parent and Christian you ought to have been all along.

It is unlikely your child will change overnight. He probably won't believe you are sincere at first and you'll have to prove it by your consistent godly actions and attitudes.

Then, there's the matter of those friends he's acquired while you were giving him all that excessive freedom, before demonstrating the maturity to handle it. If you want his heart back, you must remove the outside influences that are enticing him into the world. I mean TV, school, secular music, and especially any wrong friends, which often means all friends. (It is unlikely that a rebellious teen is hanging out with great kids you approve of.)

The younger your child, the easier it will be to remove destructive outside influences. But if your child is older and hardened toward you already, it may be very difficult. Homeschool, if you are not doing so already. Move if you have to. You must use great creativity and good judgment as you eradicate destructive outside influences and replace them with your new, improved self.

Once you've got the ball rolling, keep it going. Don't despair because the going is tough. When redirecting a younger child, I would expect things to get worse before getting better. How much more so with an older child. Make firm but reasonable rules based on God's standards (not your previous ones or your child's current ones) and enforce them via preemptive vigilance combined with creative consequences. But don't let your parenting become "rules-based." It must be "heart-based" if you truly want to win back that wonderful soul who was so close to you when he or she was a toddler.

Insist on compliance with reasonable rules, but spend extensive time living a Tomato Staking lifestyle of mentoring, teaching, instilling values, imparting faith, and loving your child. Turn to God with your whole heart, then draw your child along with you into a life of discipleship to Christ.

> *He has told you, O man, what is good; and what does the LORD require of you but to do justice, to love kindness, and to walk humbly with your God?*
>
> *- Micah 6:8*

# seventeen

# AFTERWORD

*Then Hilkiah the high priest said to Shaphan the scribe, "I have found the book of the law in the house of the LORD."... And Shaphan read it in the presence of the king. And it came about when the king heard the words of the book of the law, that he tore his clothes.*

*- II Kings 22:8-11*

## Lost and Found

When I first began writing *Raising Godly Tomatoes,* I intended it only for my own children. I wanted to provide a written record of the principles and techniques I had followed in raising them. Eventually, after two decades of parenting and writing, I began sharing some of these principles and methods with others. When I did, I was stunned to find so few like-minded moms!

Newer moms not only didn't do things the way I did, but they were learning almost the opposite, practicing everything I opposed. These moms were not succeeding in their parenting and weren't enjoying their children, but were resistant to change. My advice was generally unwelcome.

Most of these moms were not Christian, so it should not have been a surprise to find them suspicious, even hostile. But as I began sharing more with Christian mothers, I was astonished to find this same secular influence among them as well. Many believing moms had no idea how to parent in a wise, godly way. All their parenting information was coming from the world and many were failing, feeling desperate and lost.

They knew their parenting skills were decidedly ineffective, but couldn't identify the problem or pursue a remedy. They wanted their children to be godly, respectful, obedient, happy, and enjoyable, but the world was proclaiming the deception that it was unreasonable to expect so much from children.

Why is the world of parenting in such sorry shape? Why don't new moms know what to do? I often think our condition parallels that of Israel in the days of Hilkiah, before the lost book of the law was discovered. Our parenting "book" has been lost. With no truth to guide us, we are groping desperately after any vain theory that comes along.

That unbelievers would consult secularists for parenting guidance is understandable. But why would Christian parents ever consider accepting the authority of secularists? The command to *"come out from among them and be separate"* certainly applies to raising our children. God's Word ought to be our source for parenting guidance, not the world and it's vain philosophies.

Tragically, most Christians have never consulted the Scriptures for the fine parenting advice found there. How ironic that we search the Scriptures for doctrinal propositions, apologetical arguments, and exegetical sermons, and ignore the rich body of content that addresses the most daunting and significant responsibility in life—the raising and nurturing of our children.

Typical of the ignorance of most Christians in this area is the woman in the following personal incident: When my oldest children were still small, I remember telling a Christian mom I knew that all we needed to know about parenting could be found in the Word of God. She dismissed my assertion as nonsense, insisting, "The Bible doesn't tell you what do to when your toddler won't stop throwing his food on the floor."

Admittedly, you are going to search the Bible in vain for specific advice on preventing toddlers from throwing food on the floor. But is the Bible really so silent about childrearing that we must consult secular sources? I don't think so. It is overflowing with childrearing advice. Every page shouts it! In addition to its doctrines and theologies, when I open my Bible I see practical, everyday advice—parenting advice.

As I wrote *Raising Godly Tomatoes,* I included many verses to demonstrate the wealth of Biblical references on childrearing. I could have included many more. In a very real sense, one might argue that the entire Bible deals with childrearing.

If every chapter reveals how God deals with His children, we, in like fashion, have the perfect model for dealing with our own children. Every verse about Christ's obedience to His Father is a prototype symbolizing how our children should be taught to obey us. Every description or demonstration of God's character set forth in Scripture tells us what to aim at as we seek prayerfully to shape and nurture the hearts of our children.

As you go about your parenting duties, look to the principles God has laid down in His Word. Read your Bible with your children in mind. As you watch your children throughout the day, observe their character to see if it reflects the character of God as revealed in His Word. Love your children as God loves you. Remember that your final goal is a godly adult whose own offspring will conform to the example of our Lord and raise his own children toward that same goal. Search the Scriptures for the knowledge of God's heart and ways and teach your children to have the same heart and ways.

We need to find our parenting book again. I pray that *Raising Godly Tomatoes* will help to revive the biblical parenting skills taught in God's Word that have been lost to recent generations.

> *"Thus says the LORD God of Israel, 'Regarding the words which you have heard, because your heart was tender and you humbled yourself before the LORD when you heard what I spoke against this place and against its inhabitants that they should become a desolation and a curse, and you have torn your clothes and wept before Me, I truly have heard you,' declares the LORD."*
>
> *- II Kings 22:18-19*